ON THE COVERS
Ebey's Landing National Historical Reserve is
the first such unit of the National Park
System. It encompasses a rural working
landscape and community on Whidbey
Island, Washington State.

Photographs by Emi Gunn, courtesy
Lys Opp-Beckman (Ebey's Landing NHR).

Ebey's Landing National Historical Reserve

Geologic Resources Inventory Report

Natural Resource Report NPS/NRSS/GRD/NRR—2011/451

National Park Service
Geologic Resources Division
PO Box 25287
Denver, CO 80225

September 2011

U.S. Department of the Interior
National Park Service
Natural Resource Stewardship and Science
Fort Collins, Colorado

The National Park Service, Natural Resource Stewardship and Science office in Fort Collins, Colorado publishes a range of reports that address natural resource topics of interest and applicability to a broad audience in the National Park Service and others in natural resource management, including scientists, conservation and environmental constituencies, and the public.

The Natural Resource Report Series is used to disseminate high-priority, current natural resource management information with managerial application. The series targets a general, diverse audience, and may contain NPS policy considerations or address sensitive issues of management applicability.

All manuscripts in the series receive the appropriate level of peer review to ensure that the information is scientifically credible, technically accurate, appropriately written for the intended audience, and designed and published in a professional manner. This report received informal peer review by subject-matter experts who were not directly involved in the collection, analysis, or reporting of the data.

Views, statements, findings, conclusions, recommendations, and data in this report do not necessarily reflect views and policies of the National Park Service, U.S. Department of the Interior. Mention of trade names or commercial products does not constitute endorsement or recommendation for use by the U.S. Government.

Printed copies of this report are produced in a limited quantity and they are only available as long as the supply lasts. This report is available from the Geologic Resources Inventory website (http://www.nature.nps.gov/geology/inventory/gre_publications.cfm) and the Natural Resource Publications Management website (http://www.nature.nps.gov/publications/nrpm/).

Please cite this publication as:

Graham, J. 2011. Ebey's Landing National Historical Reserve: geologic resources inventory report. Natural Resource Report NPS/NRSS/GRD/NRR—2011/451. National Park Service, Fort Collins, Colorado.

NPS 484/110343, September 2011

Contents

List of Figures

List of Tables

Executive Summary

This report accompanies the digital geologic map data for Ebey's Landing National Historical Reserve in Washington, produced by the Geologic Resources Division in collaboration with its partners. It contains information relevant to resource management and scientific research. This document incorporates preexisting geologic information and does not include new data or additional fieldwork.

Ebey's Landing National Historical Reserve has the distinction of being the first national historical reserve in the National Park System. Authorized in 1978, the reserve preserves and protects an unbroken historical record of Puget Sound exploration and settlement from the 19th century to the present. Located on Whidbey Island, the largest island in the conterminous United States, Ebey's Landing National Historical Reserve lies about 43 km (27 mi) north of Seattle. Members of the central Whidbey Island community work together with local, state, and federal governments to manage the reserve and to balance the needs of the community with the protection of the reserve's resources.

The reserve lies in Washington's Puget Lowland physiographic province, a broad, low-lying region between the Cascade Range to the east and the Olympic Mountains to the west. Like the San Juan Islands, the geomorphic features on Whidbey Island were shaped by continental glaciers that advanced over the Puget Lowland during the Pleistocene ice ages. Glacial and nonglacial units of clay, silt, sand, and gravel record the advance and retreat of several glaciers through the lowland. Ice from the most recent glaciation covered the area approximately 18,000 years ago. At the height of this glaciation, Whidbey Island was covered with about 1,250 m (4,100 ft) of ice. Upon melting, the glaciers left a mixture of unconsolidated sediments that reflect a variety of depositional environments including glaciomarine seafloors, deltas, fluvial outwash plains, and ice-margin and sub-glacial environments.

Shoreline and bluff erosion of these unconsolidated deposits, potable groundwater withdrawal from these units, and potential seismic activity are three geologic issues that may impact Ebey's Landing National Historical Reserve. All of the shoreline bluffs, especially those along the western shore, are subject to constant erosion by high waves during storm events. Active erosion not only causes episodic landsliding and bluff retreat, but also affects archaeological sites. The most common American Indian archaeological sites on Whidbey Island are shell middens, the majority of which are found along marine shorelines in unconsolidated sediments. Most of these sites on Whidbey Island are actively eroding.

The primary recharge mechanism for the groundwater system on Whidbey Island is the percolation of precipitation through the heterogeneous glacial and nonglacial deposits. Because Whidbey Island lies in the rain shadow of the Olympic Mountains, less precipitation falls than expected, and most is lost to runoff, transpiration by plants, or evaporation. Percolation is further hindered by layers of low-permeability glacial sediments.

The potential for saltwater intrusion of Whidbey Island's sole source groundwater aquifer complicates the groundwater system, especially with respect to the growing population of the island and increased demand for freshwater. Saltwater contamination has been documented in the reserve and will continue to replace freshwater if pumping exceeds the rate of aquifer recharge. Development on the island may negatively impact the aquifer through increased saltwater intrusion and the introduction of nitrates, pesticides, and other contaminants.

Whidbey Island lies in an active tectonic area, and co-seismic tectonic land-level change has been documented within Ebey's Landing National Historical Reserve. The northwest-trending Southern Whidbey Island fault lies 10 km (6 mi) southeast of Admiralty Head, which forms the southwestern corner of the reserve. This fault separates two major crustal blocks and has been the source of several historic shallow earthquakes. Faults identified outside of the reserve indicate fault movement as recently as 1850 C.E. (Common Era; preferred to "A.D."). Most of Ebey's Landing National Historical Reserve is pastoral, but tectonic land-level changes and ground shaking from earthquakes are potential hazards to the historic buildings in Coupeville, the second oldest town in Washington and the commercial center of the reserve. Coupeville is built over clayey glaciomarine drift, which may not provide a firm foundation in the event of an earthquake.

Glaciers shaped the landforms on Whidbey Island and laid the foundation for the cultural history preserved at Ebey's Landing National Historical Reserve. For example, the bluffs along the western shoreline provided an excellent vantage point for Fort Casey, built in the late 1890s and currently preserved as a state park. Glacial till formed the rolling hills and agricultural lands of the San de Fuca Uplands. The clayey glaciomarine drift and gentle slopes left behind by the ice provided rich soils for the crops grown by American Indians and present-day farmers in Ebey's Prairie, located in the central portion of the reserve. Smith Prairie formed as a well-drained, elevated, and flat glaciolacustrine delta surface that was an attractive site for the location of the Coupeville airfield. The embayment of Penn Cove, which provides a naturally sheltered harbor for Coupeville and is an ideal location for the cultivation of mussels, resulted from fast-flowing, pressurized subglacial meltwater that carved a trough into the sediments between Coupeville and the uplands to the north. The formation of kettle ponds by the melting of stagnant ice shaped the landscape in the Kettle and Pratt Woodlands surrounding Fort Ebey State Park.

This report includes a Map Unit Properties Table that describes characteristics such as erosion resistance, suitability for infrastructure development, geologic significance, recreation potential, and associated cultural and mineral resources for each geologic unit mapped in Ebey's Landing National Historical Reserve.

This report also provides a glossary, which contains explanations of technical, geologic terms, including those used on the Map Unit Properties Table. Additionally, a geologic timescale (fig. 21) shows the chronological arrangement of major geologic events, with the oldest events and time units at the bottom and the youngest at the top.

Acknowledgements

The Geologic Resources Inventory (GRI) is one of 12 inventories funded by the National Park Service Inventory and Monitoring Program. The GRI is administered by the Geologic Resources Division of the Natural Resource Stewardship and Science Directorate.

The Geologic Resources Division relies heavily on partnerships with institutions such as the U.S. Geological Survey, Colorado State University, state geologic surveys, local museums, and universities in developing GRI products.

Special thanks to: Michael Polenz (Washington State DNR) supplied a draft copy of the geologic field trip guide of the reserve as well as many of the photographs used in the report. Lys Opp-Beckman (Ebey's Landing NHR) also provided images used on the covers and within the report.

Credits

Author
John P. Graham (Colorado State University)

Review
Michael Polenz (Washington State Department of Natural Resources)
Pat Pringle (Centralia College [Washington State])
Jason Kenworthy (NPS Geologic Resources Division)

Editing
Jennifer Piehl (Write Science Right)

Digital Geologic Data Production
Greg Mack (NPS Pacific West Region)
Stephanie O'Meara (Colorado State University)

Digital Geologic Data Overview Layout Design
Derek Witt (Colorado State University intern)
Philip Reiker (NPS Geologic Resources Division)
Georgia Hybels (NPS Geologic Resources Division)

Introduction

The following section briefly describes the National Park Service Geologic Resources Inventory and the regional geologic setting of Ebey's Landing National Historical Reserve.

Purpose of the Geologic Resources Inventory

The Geologic Resources Inventory (GRI) is one of 12 inventories funded by the National Park Service (NPS) Inventory and Monitoring Program. The GRI, administered by the Geologic Resources Division of the Natural Resource Stewardship and Science Directorate, is designed to provide and enhance baseline information available to park managers. The GRI team relies heavily on partnerships with institutions such as the U.S. Geological Survey, Colorado State University, state geologic surveys, local museums, and universities in developing GRI products.

The goals of the GRI are to increase understanding of the geologic processes at work in parks and to provide sound geologic information for use in park decision making. Sound park stewardship requires an understanding of the natural resources and their role in the ecosystem. Park ecosystems are fundamentally shaped by geology. The compilation and use of natural resource information by park managers is called for in section 204 of the National Parks Omnibus Management Act of 1998 and in NPS-75, Natural Resources Inventory and Monitoring Guideline.

To realize these goals, the GRI team is systematically conducting a scoping meeting for each of the 270 identified natural area parks and providing a park-specific digital geologic map and geologic report. These products support the stewardship of park resources and are designed for nongeoscientists. Scoping meetings bring together park staff and geologic experts to review available geologic maps and discuss specific geologic issues, features, and processes.

The GRI mapping team converts the geologic maps identified for park use at the scoping meeting into digital geologic data in accordance with their Geographic Information Systems (GIS) Data Model. These digital data sets bring an interactive dimension to traditional paper maps. The digital data sets provide geologic data for use in park GIS and facilitate the incorporation of geologic considerations into a wide range of resource management applications. The newest maps contain interactive help files. This geologic report assists park managers in the use of the map and provides an overview of park geology and geologic resource management issues.

For additional information regarding the content of this report and current GRI contact information please refer to the Geologic Resources Inventory website (http://www.nature.nps.gov/geology/inventory/).

Significance of Ebey's Landing National Historical Reserve

Located on Whidbey Island at the entrance to Puget Sound, Ebey's Landing National Historical Reserve is the nation's first historical reserve (fig. 1). Public concern over the intent to develop three residential subdivisions on Ebey's Prairie and adjoining farmland—nearly half of Whidbey Island's total area—prompted Congress to establish the reserve in 1978 to preserve and protect the cultural landscape and to commemorate the history of a rural community. Ebey's Landing National Historical Reserve provides a vivid and continuous historical record of exploration and American settlement in the Puget Sound region from the 19th century to the present.

Most of the acreage included in the reserve is privately owned; only 1,096.18 ha (2,708.73 ac) of the reserve's 7,820.14 ha (19,323.99 ac) are federal (National Park Service 2004). The reserve contains two state parks, Fort Casey and Fort Ebey, and more than 6,500 pieces of private property, including the town of Coupeville, the county seat for Island County (Dietrich 2004). Because so much of the land was privately owned, the enabling legislation established the reserve as a non-traditional National Park Service unit to be managed by a unit of local government. To meet this requirement, the Trust Board of Ebey's Landing National Historical Reserve was formed to manage the reserve. The National Park Service, local and state governments, and the residents of the central Whidbey Island community work collaboratively to help balance the needs of the community with the protection of the reserve's resources.

Although the Puget Sound region is experiencing rapid economic development, Ebey's Landing National Historical Reserve provides a broad spectrum of Northwest history that remains clearly visible within a large-scale (and partially protected) landscape. Rich prairie soils are still being farmed, forests are being harvested, and historic buildings are being used as homes or places of business just as they were a century ago, when New England sea captains were drawn to Penn Cove.

Regional Description

Whidbey Island is located about 43 km (27 mi) north of Seattle and 80 km (50 mi) south of the Canadian border. Extending nearly 64 km (40 mi) north-south and 1.6–16 km (1–10 mi) east-west, Whidbey is the largest island not only in Puget Sound but also in the conterminous United States (fig. 2; National Park Service 2000). Like most

Puget Sound landforms, Whidbey Island is no higher than 150 m (500 ft) in elevation (fig. 3).

Ebey's Landing National Historical Reserve occupies a narrow bend in central Whidbey Island. Approximately 42% of the land is classified as "agricultural/open space" by Island County and is contained primarily within Smith, Crockett, and Ebey's prairies (National Park Service 2000). Ebey's Prairie is the largest open space in the reserve and contains the most productive agricultural land. About 36% of the reserve is classified as woodlands, 11.4% as residential, nearly 5% as wetland, and 1% as urban commercial space.

The reserve has been divided into ten cultural landscape areas, recognizable by their distinctive landforms and critical landscape components (Gilbert, 1985; National Park Service 2006). The connection between the geology of the island and these cultural landscapes is described in the Features and Processes section.

Geologic Setting

Ebey's Landing National Historical Reserve lies within the Puget Lowland physiographic province, a broad, low-lying region between the Cascade Range and the Olympic Mountains (Easterbrook 1994; Dragovich et al. 2005). Similar to most of the Puget Lowland, Ebey's Landing National Historical Reserve contains abundant glacial sediments and no bedrock exposures (fig. 4). Thick unconsolidated deposits cover bedrock that is possibly Miocene in age (23–5 million years ago) and lies about 350–790 m (1,150–2,600 ft) below the surface (fig. 5). The oldest sediment exposed in the area is the 185,000(?)–125,000-year-old Double Bluff Drift [map unit Qgd(d)], which crops out at beach level south of Ebey's Landing.

Glacial and interglacial units on Whidbey Island record the advance and retreat of glaciers during the Pleistocene ice ages. The most recent glacial advances occurred approximately 18,000 and 14,000 years ago, during a period known as the Vashon Stade of the Fraser Glaciation (Burns 1985; Polenz et al. 2005; Washington State Department of Natural Resources 2010). A "stade" is a substage of a glacial stage. During the Vashon Stade glacial maximum, Whidbey Island was covered with about 1,250 m (4,100 ft) of ice. The Vashon Till [map unit Qgt(v)], a deposit of poorly sorted boulder-clay, was left when the glaciers melted.

Most of the upland areas of Whidbey Island and Camano Island, which lies between Whidbey Island and the mainland, are covered by Vashon Till. The till varies in thickness from less than one meter to approximately 53 m (175 ft) and covers outwash sands [map unit Qga(v)] that were also deposited during the Vashon Stade. The till is overlain by glaciomarine drift gravels deposited about 13,500 years ago during the Everson Interstade (fig. 4). Glaciomarine drift is a general term for any rock material that was deposited in a marine environment by a glacier, a pro-glacial debris flow, or an ice berg.

Other features that record glacial processes at Ebey's Landing National Historical Reserve include drumlins (elongate oval hills or ridges of compacted glacial till) and kettle ponds (fig. 6), which formed in steep-walled depressions exceeding 60 m (200ft) in depth that were left behind when large, soil-covered blocks of glacial ice melted.

Although no tectonic faults have been mapped onshore, the reserve area is tectonically active. Tectonic land-level changes may occur due to movement along the northwest-trending Southern Whidbey Island fault, which lies 10 km (6 mi) southeast of Admiralty Head (Polenz et al. 2005). This fault has produced shallow crustal earthquakes in the Quaternary and is capable of generating large earthquakes with surface-wave magnitudes of 7 or greater. Approximately 2,800–3,200 years ago, Crocket Lake was uplifted 1–2 m (3–7 ft) as a result of movement on the Southern Whidbey Island fault caused by a magnitude 6.5–7 earthquake (Kelsey et al. 2004).

A Holocene fault branching to the east from the Southern Whidbey Island fault may have produced the multiple north-dipping thrust faults that are exposed in pre-Vashon sediments south of Ebey's Landing. The faults do not penetrate the Vashon deposits. In the northeastern corner of the reserve, a poorly defined, northwest-trending pre-Vashon-age fault has been mapped parallel to the Oak Harbor Fault, which lies north of the reserve (Dragovich et al. 2005; Polenz et al. 2005).

North of the reserve, the Utsalady Point, Strawberry Point, and Devils Mountain faults comprise a west-trending, active, complex, transpressional deformation zone (Johnson et al. 2003; Dragovich et al. 2005; Polenz et al. 2005). The faults have uplifted Pleistocene strata in the Oak Harbor area relative to the Ebey's Landing National Historical Reserve region. Trenching along the Utsalady Point fault unearthed evidence of possible postglacial fault movement between 1550 and 1850 C.E. (Johnson et al. 2003).

Cultural History

Skagit, Snohomish, Kikalos, and Clallam tribes inhabited central Whidbey Island as early as 1300 C.E., more than 500 years before Euro-American settlers arrived. Abundant salmon, bottom fish, shellfish, berries, small game, deer, water fowl, and other natural resources encouraged the Skagit Indians to establish three permanent villages on the shores of Penn Cove at Snakelum Point, Long Point, and Monroe's Landing. They practiced selective burning, transplanting, and mulching on the prairies for the cultivation of root crops such as bracken fern, camas, and nettles. Although more than 1,500 American Indians were living in the area in 1790, the American Indian population around Coupeville had been reduced to a few small families by 1904.

In 1825, the Hudson Bay Company established Fort Vancouver on the Columbia River, which would serve as their headquarters for the Pacific region. Directors and senior officers of the Hudson Bay Company organized the Puget Sound Agricultural Company in 1840 to develop agricultural businesses and settlements in the region. Members of the Hudson Bay Company introduced the potato to Whidbey Island in the early 1800s, which resulted in the transformation of the prairies into permanent agricultural lands.

Captain George Vancouver named Whidbey Island in honor of his Lieutenant, Joseph Whidbey, who explored the island in 1792. Vancouver's exploration of Puget Sound helped prepare the way for Euro-American settlers, although the Donation Land Law of 1850 was a more significant inducement. This law offered free land in Oregon Territory to any citizen who would homestead the land for four years. Within three years, droves of settlers had carved out irregularly- shaped claims in the fertile prairies of central Whidbey Island. This early settlement pattern can still be seen today on the reserve, where it is marked by fence lines, roads, and ridges.

Colonel Isaac Neff Ebey was among the first of the permanent settlers on the island. Samuel Crockett, Ebey's friend, encouraged him leave his Missouri home and come to central Whidbey Island. Both Crockett and Ebey filed donation claims on central Whidbey in the spring of 1851. Ebey's family soon joined him. The simple home of Jacob Ebey, Isaac's father, and a blockhouse erected to defend his claim against American Indians, still stand today overlooking Ebey's Prairie.

Isaac became a leading figure in public affairs and established Ebey's Landing, an improbable seaport on the windy Strait of Juan de Fuca where Ebey landed goods before carrying them up a ravine to his ferry house. Isaac's contributions to the community were cut short, however, when Haida Indians decapitated him in 1857 in revenge for the killing of one of their chieftains.

Some farmers still cultivate the rich alluvial soil on donation land claims established by their families in the 1850s, preserving a centuries-old historic land-use pattern. However, fertile farmland was not the only incentive to settle on Whidbey Island. The protective harbor of Penn Cove and the stands of tall timber valued for shipbuilding lured sea captains and merchants from New England to the island. These pioneers established donation claims along the shoreline.

One colorful sea captain who made his home on central Whidbey Island was Thomas Coupe, who amazed his peers by sailing a full-rigged ship through treacherous Deception Pass on the northern end of the island. In 1852, Coupe claimed 320 acres on the south shore of Penn Cove. The town of Coupeville was later built on his claim.

Coupeville became a dominant seaport due to the early success of central Whidbey's farming and maritime trade. Traces of its lively past remain visible today in the many 19th-century false-fronted commercial buildings on Front Street, the historic wharf and blockhouse, and the rich collection of Victorian residential architecture. Whidbey Island became home to a thriving Chinese community between the 1880s and the 1920s. The community centered on Ebey's Prairie farmlands, where the Chinese became indispensable farmhands for local white families. Like elsewhere in the American West, however, the Chinese were often treated as unwelcome outsiders. Fear that Chinese laborers would take jobs from white workers led to a series of political and social movements that targeted Chinese communities like the one on Whidbey Island.

Beginning in 1882, exclusion acts prevented most Chinese laborers from entering the country. Chinese merchants and laborers on Whidbey Island faced increasing hostility, intimidation, and violence from their neighbors. Anti-Chinese activities, spearheaded by the white business owners of Coupeville in the 1890s, and virulent anti-Chinese editorials targeted Chinese residents of Ebey's Prairie and other island communities. Unidentified vigilantes dynamited piles of harvested potatoes awaiting sale and shot the windows out of Chinese houses under the cover of night.

Some Chinese took up arms to defend themselves, others enlisted the vocal support of white neighbors and employers, and some simply moved on, leaving Ebey's Prairie permanently. By the late 1920s, the last aging Chinese residents of Ebey's Prairie had moved off the island, returned to China, or died. Only scattered evidence remained of the 200 Chinese individuals who once made their home on Whidbey Island. Ah Soot, a Chinese emigrant who came to the United States in 1880 and died in 1925, is buried in Sunnyside Cemetery and is the only known Chinese resident of Whidbey Island who chose not to make the final journey back to China for a traditional burial alongside his ancestors.

The military introduced another layer of island history with the construction of Fort Casey Military Reservation in the late 1890s. The fort was built on the bluff above Admiralty Head as part of a three-fort defense system designed to protect the entrance to Puget Sound. U.S. Army troops reported for duty in 1900, and 400 troops had been stationed at Fort Casey by 1910. Fort Casey became a social center for the surrounding community. The wood-framed officers' quarters, gun escarpments, Admiralty Head Lighthouse, and other military remnants can still be seen at old Fort Casey.

Fort Ebey, a remnant of the defensive build-up of World War II, stands near the northern boundary of the reserve. South of the fort, Navy pilots continue to use the 1943 Coupeville Outlying Landing Field for aircraft carrier landing practice.

Authorized in 1978, Ebey's Landing National Historical Reserve preserves and protects an unbroken historical record of Puget Sound exploration and settlement from the 19th century to the present. From the historical farms that are still under cultivation today to the Victorian seaport community of Coupeville, the reserve protects a cultural landscape that connects the past and present   spirits of the island.

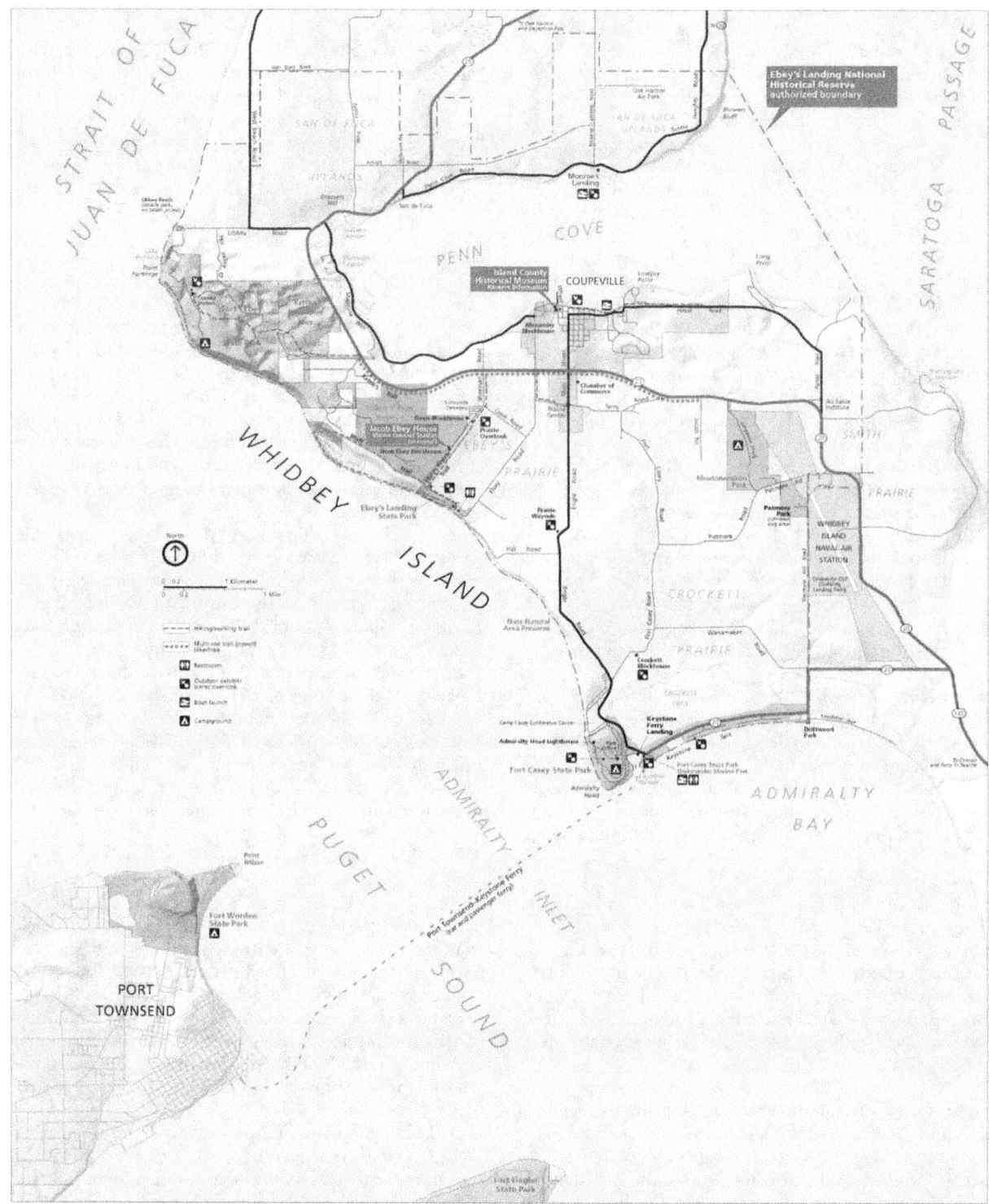

Figure 1. Location map of Ebey's Landing National Historical Reserve. National Park Service map available online: http://home.nps.gov/applications/hafe/hfc/carto-detail.cfm?Alpha=EBLA, accessed September 13, 2011.

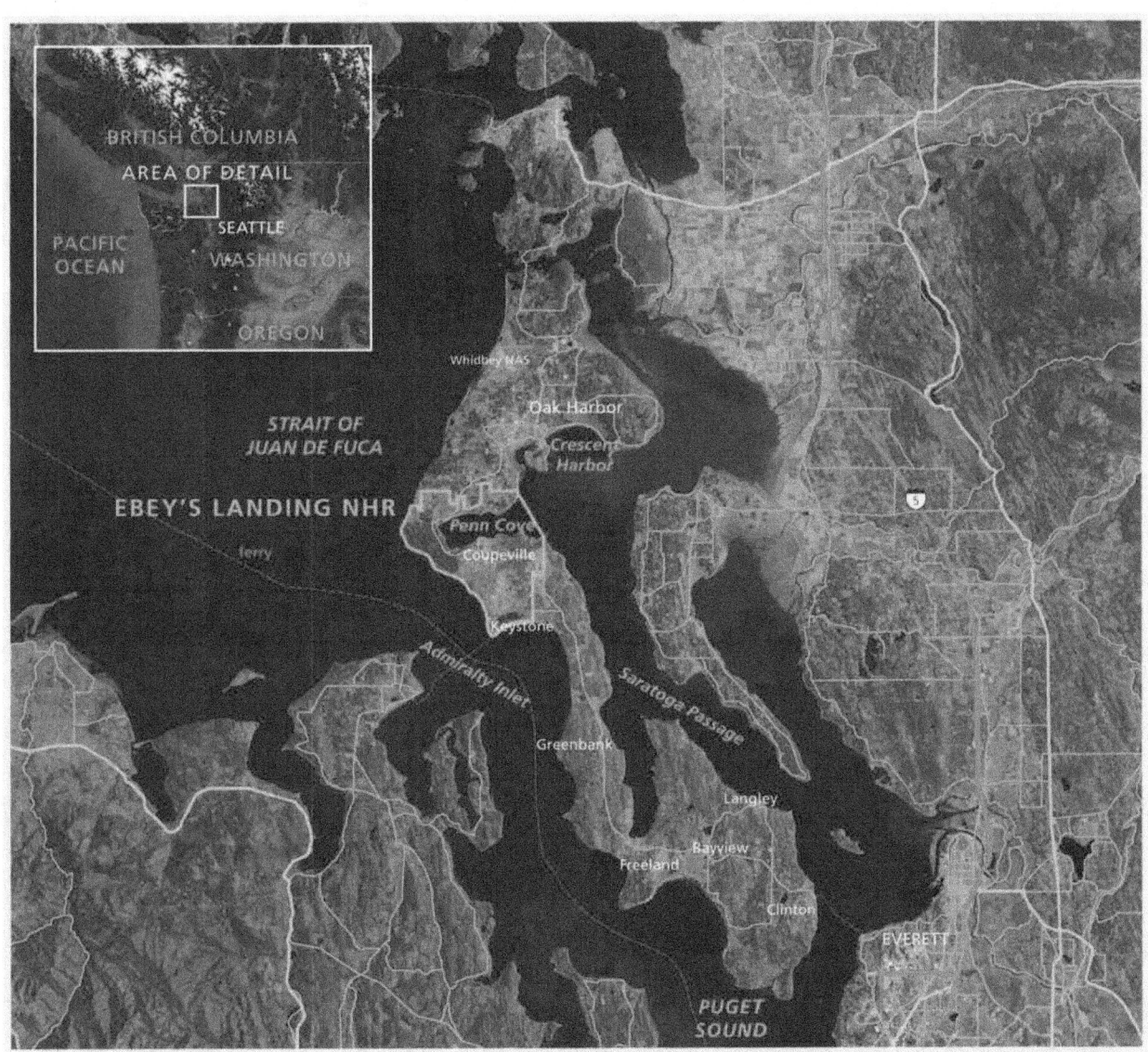

Figure 2. Whidbey Island, the "C-shaped" island in the middle of the image lies approximately 48 km (30 mi) north of Seattle and forms the northern boundary of Puget Sound. The island is approximately 56 km (35 mi) long and 2.4–19 km (1.5–12 mi) wide. Map compiled by Jason Kenworthy (NPS Geologic Resources Division) from ESRI World Imagery basemap.

Figure 3. Whidbey Island. Although the maximum elevation is only 150 m (500 ft), the western bluffs of Whidbey Island rise abruptly along the coastline and are susceptible to erosion and bluff retreat. Photograph courtesy Michael Polenz (Washington Department of Natural Resources).

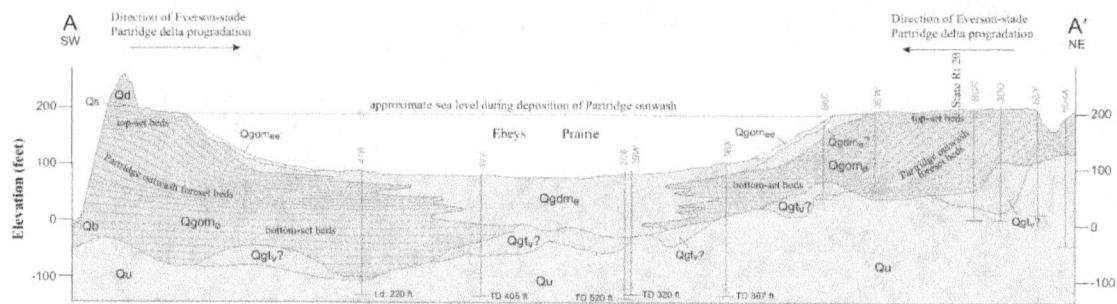

Lithologic Units		
Post-glacial Deposits		
Qd	Dune deposits	Qb	Beach deposits
Deposits of the Fraser Glaciation		
Everson Interstade		*Vashon Stade*
Qgom(ee)	Glaciomarine drift, beach	Qgt(v)	Till
Qgdm(e)	Glaciomarine drift, undivided		
Qgom(e)	Partridge Gravel		
Qu	Pleistocene deposits, undivided		

Figure 4. This southwest-to-northeast geologic cross-section A–A' from Polenz et al. (2005; see Geologic Map Overview Graphic) illustrates the thick sequence of glacial deposits and lack of bedrock in Ebey's Landing National Historical Reserve. Vertical exaggeration is 10 times. Note the relatively flat topography formed by the deltaic and channel outwash deposits of the Partridge Gravel. This well-drained, flat topography became the preferred site for the Coupeville airport. The wells that are shown are from the Island County well database. TD is the total depth of the well. Map units are the same as those found on the Map Unit Properties Table and the enclosed GIS map. The location of the cross-section is also on the Geologic Map Overview Graphic. Cross section from Polenz et al. (2005).

Epoch	Age (thousands of years before present)	Stratigraphic Units (map symbols)	General description of units
Late Pleistocene - Holocene	12.69–present	Postglacial deposits Qf, Qml, Qb, Qd, Qp, Qm, Qmw, Qls, Qs	Marsh, peat, mass wasting, and dune (>9,000 years BP to recent) deposits.
Pleistocene	13.65–12.69	Glaciomarine sediments of Everson Interstade Qgom(ee), Qmf(e), Qgdm(e), Qgdm(els), Qgos(e), Qgim(e)	Glaciomarine drift (gravel, sand, silt, clay); fan deposits; landslide deposits; ice-marginal moraine deposits.
		Partridge Gravel Qgom(e), Qgog(e)	Sand, gravel, sand-gravel mixtures.
	~18	Vashon Drift Qgt(v), Qgt(va), Qga(v)	Unsorted, unstratified till (loose gravel, sand, silt, and clay); outwash sand and gravel.
	~60–18	Olympia Nonglacial Interval Qc(o)	Silt, clay, sand, interbeds of fine gravel
	~80–60	Possession Drift Qgd(p)	Glaciomarine drift, till, outwash sand
	~125–80	Whidbey Formation Qc(w)	Sand, silt, clay, peat layers
	≥185–125	Double Bluff Drift Qgd(d)	Silt, clay, diamicton glaciomarine drift
Pliocene	Regional unconformity (a break or gap in the stratigraphic succession of rock units)		
Miocene			
	5,330	Not exposed	Bedrock at depth

Figure 5. General stratigraphic column for Ebey's Landing National Historical Reserve. Ages (in thousands of years before 1950) are taken from Polenz et al. (2005). Detailed descriptions of each unit can be found in the Map Unit Properties Table.

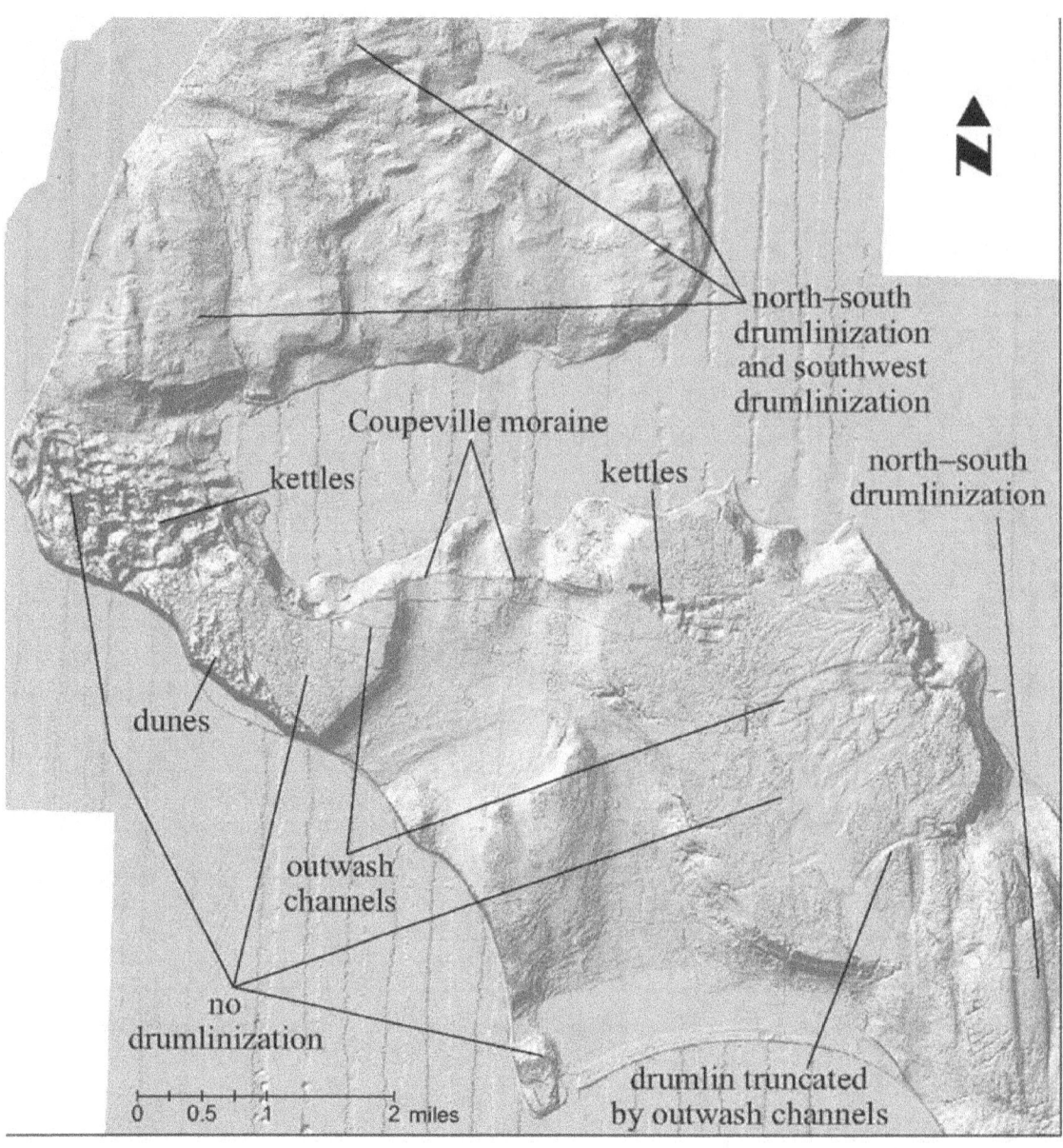

Figure 6. Lidar-based image of glacial features associated with Ebey's Landing National Historical Reserve. Well-defined, north–south drumlins in the southeast record the southerly ice movement during the Vashon Stade. In the north, less-defined north–south drumlins are overprinted by southwest-trending drumlinization, which records southern ice movement followed by southwestern ice movement. The Coupeville moraine reflects a former ice margin. East and west of the moraine, outwash channels and kettles record the ice-proximal, marine-deltaic deposition of the Partridge Gravel. The smooth lowlands north and south of the Coupeville moraine represent the ancient sea floor. Vertical exaggeration is 6 times. Image courtesy Michael Polenz (Washington Department of Natural Resources). LIDAR data by David Finlayson (University of Washington).

Geologic Issues

The Geologic Resources Division held a Geologic Resources Inventory scoping session for Ebey's Landing National Historical Reserve on September 10-12, 2002, to discuss geologic resources, address the status of geologic mapping, and assess resource management issues and needs. This section synthesizes the scoping results, in particular those issues that may require attention from resource managers. Contact the Geologic Resources Division for technical assistance.

Significant geologic issues facing resource managers at Ebey's Landing National Historical Reserve were identified during the 2002 scoping meeting. The issues involve eroding bluffs and the protection of sustainable groundwater resources. Shoreline erosion causes bluff retreat and also negatively impacts archaeological resources on Whidbey Island (National Park Service 2008).

Other potential hazards include seismic (earthquake) and volcanic activity. The Southern Whidbey Island fault is tectonically active and has been the source of several historic, shallow crustal earthquakes. This fault has the potential to generate earthquakes with surface-wave magnitudes of 7 or greater (Polenz et al. 2005). In the past, volcanic activity from Glacier Peak in the Cascade Range has impacted the area of the reserve. In addition to these issues, global climate change may cause issues associated with relative sea level rise and the increased erosion of coastal bluffs.

Shoreline Erosion and Bluff Retreat

The shoreline along the western margin of Whidbey Island erodes at an approximate rate of 0.3 m (1 ft) per year (Keuler 1988; Shipman 2004). High waves during storms destroy the seaward edge of the beach face and batter the bluffs along the western shore (fig. 7). When the base of the bluffs is undercut, the bluffs collapse, generating the mass-wasting (map unit Qmw) and landslide deposits (map unit Ql) that appear on the park's geologic map (see Geologic Map Data section). All of the shoreline bluffs are susceptible to episodic landsliding and resultant bluff retreat (fig. 8). Most slide deposits, however, are quickly removed by wave action (Polenz 2005). Global climate change may also increase bluff erosion (see below). Increased winter rainfall and relative sea level rise will negatively impact already unstable slopes (Karl et al. 2009).

Active erosion affects shell middens, the most common American Indian archaeological site on Whidbey Island. These sites are the remains of subsistence activities conducted a few hundred to a few thousand years ago. The majority of central Whidbey Island's shell midden sites are found along marine shorelines, and most of these sites are actively eroding. Shoreline erosion may eventually destroy most of these middens (National Park Service 2008).

In Island County, approximately 50% of the shoreline has been designated as unstable (Shipman 2004; Klinger et al. 2007). Wieczorek and Snyder (2009) described various types of slope movements and triggering mechanisms for mass-wasting processes and suggested five significant properties, or vital signs, that could be used to monitor slope movements. These vital signs included: 1) type of landslide, 2) landslide triggers and causes, 3) geologic material components, 4) landslide movement, and 5) landslide hazards and risks. Although these vital signs are associated primarily with mass movement in bedrock terrain, they may be applicable to the monitoring of mass-wasting and landslide potential along the steep shoreline bluffs of Ebey's Landing National Historical Reserve.

Bush and Young (2009) delineated vital signs that can be used to provide insight into the general state of a coastal ecosystem, changes in the system, and the vitality of the system. These vital signs included: 1) shoreline change, 2) coastal dune geomorphology, 3) coastal vegetation cover, 4) topography/elevation, 5) composition of beach material, 6) wetland position/acreage, and 7) coastal wetland accretion. They also provided detailed monitoring techniques and recommendations for resource managers, including a description of the necessary expertise, personnel, and equipment, approximate cost, and labor intensity.

Reserve resource managers may consider implementing these various monitoring strategies in order to mitigate bluff erosion and its impact to archaeological sites.

Groundwater Resources

The unconsolidated sediments in Ebey's Landing National Historical Reserve contain an aquifer with a finite water supply that begins at a depth slightly above sea level and extends to about 61 m (200 ft) below sea level (Klinger et al. 2007). This aquifer is referred to as the sea level aquifer, and it is the sole source of domestic and agricultural water for the area. Because it is the only aquifer on the island, the government of Island County requested and received from the U.S. Environmental Protection Agency the designation as a Sole Source Aquifer in 1982. The designation provides for a high level of regulatory protection and an additional review of any federally funded projects to ensure that there will be no degradation to the county's aquifer system (National Park Service 2006).

The groundwater system is recharged by precipitation, although most precipitation is lost to runoff, transpiration by plants, or evaporation. Less precipitation than might be expected falls on Whidbey Island because it lies in the rain shadow of the Olympic Mountains, which stand between the Pacific Coast and the island. Because of the rain shadow effect, an annual average of only 0.5 m (1.6 ft) of rain falls in the vicinity of Coupeville, in comparison with the 3.7 m (12 ft) of annual rainfall received by the west-facing valleys of Olympic National Park.

Surface permeability also influences groundwater recharge. Glacial sediments containing abundant clay have low permeability and impede vertical groundwater flow to the aquifer.

The withdrawal of groundwater for domestic, agricultural, and commercial use exceeds the recharge of the aquifer in the vicinity of Ebey's Landing National Historical Reserve. As a result, saltwater has intruded into the freshwater aquifer in some areas. Saltwater contamination has been documented within the reserve in the areas of West Beach, Coupeville, Ebey's Prairie, and outside the reserve at Admiral's Cove (National Park Service 2006). Since the aquifer can remain salty for an extended period once contaminated, preventive management of the aquifer is more effective and efficient than remedial measures.

Increased water demand as a result of population growth and accompanying development has the potential to negatively impact groundwater recharge areas and to increase groundwater contamination. Saltwater intrusion and the introduction of nitrates, pesticides, and other contaminants may negatively impact the sea level aquifer. In 2007, the Water Resources Division of the National Park Service recommended that the reserve develop measures "to protect and preserve the sea level aquifer under coastal development and climate change scenarios" (Klinger et al. 2007, p. 87). Additional information regarding these measures is beyond the scope of this report, but may be obtained by contacting the Water Resources Division of the National Park Service in Fort Collins, Colorado.

Seismic (Earthquake) Potential

Although no tectonic faults have been mapped on Whidbey Island, gravity, aeromagnetic, and well data have been used to infer a northwest-trending fault, called the Southern Whidbey Island fault, which may have moved since the Pleistocene Ice Age (Gower 1980). The fault crosses southern Whidbey Island near Lagoon Point, about 10 km (6 mi) southeast of Admiralty Head. It enters the Coupeville quadrangle about 3 km (2 mi) south of Admiralty Head and extends to the west of Point Partridge (Wagner and Wiley 1980). The Southern Whidbey Island fault has been characterized as a broad (6–11 km; 4–7 mi), long-lived, transpressional zone that trends northwest (310°), dips near-vertically to steeply north-northeast, and can be traced for over 69 km (43

mi) (Johnson et al. 1996). Despite the absence of recognized fault strands, future earthquakes associated with this fault zone could produce surface rupture within the reserve area (Michael Polenz, Geologist, Washington Department of Natural Resources, written communication, March 2011).

The Southern Whidbey Island fault separates two major crustal blocks and has been the source of several historic shallow crustal earthquakes. It is capable of generating magnitude 7 or greater earthquakes (Johnson et al. 1996). Data from trenching investigations in 2005 record four to possibly eight postglacial earthquakes along the fault zone, making it one of the most active shallow crustal faults documented in the Puget Lowland (Polenz et al. 2005). The 1–2 m (3–7 ft) uplift of Crocket Lake that occurred 2,800–3,200 years ago has been attributed to a 6.5–7 magnitude earthquake in the Southern Whidbey Island fault zone (Kelsey et al. 2004).

An upright log, possibly a Douglas fir, discovered in the intertidal zone at the northwestern end of Penn Cove provides evidence of previous tectonic subsidence (Polenz 2005). The log has a diameter of approximately 0.40 m (1.3 ft) including the bark and is heavily bored by clams (fig. 9). Data from subsurface cores indicate a minimum subsidence of 1.4 m (4.5 ft). Preliminary data from historical records and radiocarbon dating suggest that the log was rapidly submerged by a tectonic event that occurred between 1740 and 1790 C.E. or between 1810 and 1850 C.E. (Polenz 2005).

The Utsalady Point, Strawberry Point, and Devils Mountain fault zones have been mapped a few kilometers north of the reserve (Johnson et al. 2001; Dragovich et al. 2005). These three west-trending fault zones comprise a complex transpressional deformation zone that has uplifted Pleistocene strata in the Oak Harbor area relative to strata in the reserve.

Evidence from trenching in the Utsalady Point fault zone suggests postglacial fault movement between 1550 and 1850 C.E. (Johnson et al. 2003). The submerged log excavated at the northwestern end of Penn Cove may have been tectonically lowered into the intertidal zone as a result of this tectonic activity. The deformation event may have tilted the strata north of Penn Cove slightly to the south.

Another Holocene fault may extend east from the Southern Whidbey Island fault to the shore south of Ebey's Landing. In this area, multiple north-dipping thrusts are exposed in pre-Vashon sediments, but the faults do not appear to penetrate the Vashon deposits (Wagner and Wiley 1980).

Other faults have been mapped and inferred north of the reserve. The southeastern end of a poorly defined, northwest-trending, possibly pre-Vashon-aged fault is inferred to pass through the northeastern corner of Ebey's Landing National Historical Reserve, and another northwest-trending fault, the Oak Harbor Fault, has been mapped north of this probable pre-Vashon structure (Dragovich et al. 2005).

The town of Coupeville is built on glaciomarine drift composed primarily of silt and clay [map unit Qgdm(e)]. Possible liquefaction features in Pleistocene deposits (map unit Qu) along the shoreline of Penn Cove, west of Long Point, suggest movement from previous earthquakes. Ground shaking from earthquakes may present a hazard to historical buildings which were not engineered to withstand earthquakes.

Seismographs record earthquakes and many of them automatically send their data to centralized locations for routine analysis. The U.S. Geological Survey maintains an earthquake website (http://earthquake.usgs.gov, accessed June 1, 2011) that contains historical and near-real-time data, as well as links to regional information. The Pacific Northwest Seismic Network (http://www.pnsn.org/, accessed June 1, 2011) provides information on Pacific Northwest earthquake activity and hazards and operates seismographs in Washington and Oregon. These websites can provide up-to-date information on seismic activity affecting Whidbey Island and Ebey's Landing National Historical Reserve.

Glacier Peak Eruptive Potential

Glacier Peak lies approximately 110 km (70 mi) northeast of Seattle. Although Glacier Peak is a relatively short (3,213 m; 10,541 ft) volcanic peak in the Cascade Range, since the retreat of the ice-age glaciers approximately 15,000 years ago, it has produced more explosive eruptions with voluminous volcanic ash content than any other Washington volcano except Mount St. Helens (Waitt et al. 1995; U.S. Geological Survey 2008). Glacier Peak and Mount St. Helens are the only Washington volcanoes to produce large, explosive ash eruptions.

At Blowers Bluff (fig. 10), the Whidbey Formation [map unit Qc(w)], which was deposited between 125,000 and 80,000 years ago, contains pebbles from a lahar (volcanic mudflow) generated by the Glacier Peak volcano (Polenz 2005; Polenz et al. 2005). The lahar flowed into the area currently demarcated by Ebey's Landing National Historical Reserve because neither Skagit Bay nor the Saratoga Passage existed at the time (Polenz 2005).

Since the retreat of glacial ice, Glacier Peak has produced only two major eruptions: one between 13,100 and 12,500 years ago and another between 6,300 and 5,900 years ago. Smaller eruptions that produce small amounts of ash and lahars of limited areal extent occur more frequently than these larger eruptions. In the past 2,000 years, Glacier Peak has generated at least seven smaller eruptions (U.S. Geological Survey 2008).

Should another large eruption occur from Glacier Peak, lahars present the greatest danger to communities located near the volcano (Waitt et al. 1995; U.S. Geological Survey 2008). Today, Skagit Bay eliminates the potential lahar hazard to Ebey's Landing National Historical Reserve. Airborne ash, the second greatest

hazard from a large Glacier Peak eruption, might impact Whidbey Island, but most of the ash would be carried eastward by the prevailing wind (Waitt et al. 1995). Should Glacier Peak erupt, earthquakes would accompany the eruption, although the potential extent of ground shaking is difficult to determine. Although relatively minor, the potential for ground shaking and ash fall from large Glacier Peak eruptions exists for Ebey's Landing National Historical Reserve.

The U.S. Geological Survey Cascades Volcano Observatory website (http://vulcan.wr.usgs.gov/, accessed June 1, 2011) contains detailed information on the volcanoes in the Cascade Range, including Glacier Peak. The website contains information on potential volcanic hazards and related publications, photographs, and current news releases. It also provides links to other relevant websites.

Climate Change

The Puget Sound region is expected to experience a number of impacts in the next 50–100 years due to climate change. Sea-level in the Puget Sound basin may rise 33 cm (13 in) or more by 2100, depending on the rate of ice melt from Greenland and Antarctica and local vertical land movement caused by isostatic rebound and tectonic subduction (Klinger et al. 2007; Karl et al. 2009). The projected heavier winter rainfall in the Puget Sound region will combine with rising sea level to increase erosion along the exposed bluffs facing Admiralty Inlet. Bluff recession typically results from the removal of material from the base of the bluff by wave action, causing the subsequent collapse of the unstable bluff slope. Rising sea level, an increase in rainfall intensity and frequency, and a corresponding increase in storm surges will combine to increase bluff erosion and retreat, particularly along the western coast of Whidbey Island (Klinger et al. 2007).

Rising sea level will also inundate low-lying coastal areas, including wetlands, and change the salinity of semi-enclosed bays, such as Penn Cove. Rising sea level may eliminate Perego's, Grasser's, and Kennedy's lagoons. Severe winter storms may breach Keystone Spit and negatively impact roads, campgrounds, and other infrastructure. Salt water intrusion into the sea-level aquifer will increase (Canning 2002; Klinger et al. 2007).

In the Pacific Northwest, warmer, wetter winters followed by warmer summers will reduce the flow of freshwater in summer and increase water flow in fall and winter. These changes will impact the rates of aquifer recharge, soil saturation, and seawater intrusion into the sea-level aquifer. Frequent water shortages can be expected in summer. Projections of population growth and residential and commercial development in the vicinity of Ebey's Landing National Historical Reserve are needed to assess the potential magnitude of these impacts associated with climate change (Klinger et al. 2007).

Other Issues

Tsunamis

Some areas within Ebey's Landing National Historical Reserve may be vulnerable to inundation from tsunamis generated by earthquakes along the Cascadia Subduction Zone, which lies off the coast of Washington, Oregon, and northern California. Keystone Spit, Crockett Lake, and the Admiralty Bay shoreline could be inundated to levels of 0.5–2 m (1.6–6.6 ft). Kennedy's Lagoon, Mueller Point, and Long Point in Penn Cove may be inundated to similar levels (Walsh et al. 2005).

Earthquakes generated along the Cascadia Subduction Zone occur, on average, about every 500 to 540 years (Atwater and Hemphill-Haley 1997; Walsh et al. 2005). The characteristic magnitude of earthquakes along the subduction zone is not known, but the last earthquake, which occurred in 1700, has been estimated to have been a Richter scale magnitude 9 earthquake (Satake et al. 1996, 2003; Walsh et al. 2005).

Elwha Dam Removal

The nation's largest dam removal project began in September 2011 in the Elwha Valley on the Olympic Peninsula, west of Ebey's Landing National Historical Reserve. The project will remove two dams on the Elwha River that were built in 1910 and 1926. The Elwha watershed is the largest watershed in Olympic National Park, and restoration will return the river to its natural free-flowing state. More than 113 km (70 mi) of river will be restored, benefitting all five species of Pacific salmon (National Park Service 2011).

Removal of the dams will also release approximately 13 million m^3 (460 million ft^3) of sediment to downstream and nearshore areas. Most of the released sediment is expected to impact the northern shore of the Olympic Peninsula, but the entire eastern Strait of Juan de Fuca may be affected, including the western shore of Ebey's Landing Historical Reserve. If the released sediment reaches the western shore, the most probable impact will be increased sediment along some shoreline areas (Klinger et al. 2007).

Updates on the dam removal project may be found on the Olympic National Park website (http://www.nps.gov/olym/naturescience/elwha-ecosystem-restoration.htm, accessed June 3, 2011).

Oil and Fuel Spills

Ships carrying thousands of barrels of unrefined oil travel daily through Admiralty Inlet on their way to the major cargo ports of Seattle and Tacoma. Oil refineries near Anacortes and Bellingham also use shipping channels near Whidbey Island. In recent years, oil spills have occurred in Puget Sound, and future spills may impact the shoreline at Ebey's Landing National Historical Reserve.

The National Oceanic and Atmospheric Administration (NOAA) has developed a computer program, called GNOME (the General NOAA Oil Modeling Environment), that can be used to predict the path of an oil spill based on the wind, currents, and other forces (National Oceanic and Atmospheric Administration 2005). The model is most useful when an actual spill has just occurred and can be accessed on the NOAA website (http://response.restoration.noaa.gov/software/gnome/gnome.html, accessed June 7, 2011).

In addition, the Washington State Department of Ecology (2003) has developed a geographic response plan for Admiralty Inlet. The purpose of the plan is to help those who are first on the scene of an oil spill to avoid the initial confusion that is common at any spill.

Figure 7. Steep shoreline bluffs at Ebey's Landing National Historical Reserve are prone to erosion. Waves eroding the base of the bluffs cause mass wasting and landslides and then carry the material away from the shore. Photograph by Ashley Davis, courtesy Lys Opp-Beckman (Ebey's Landing NHR).

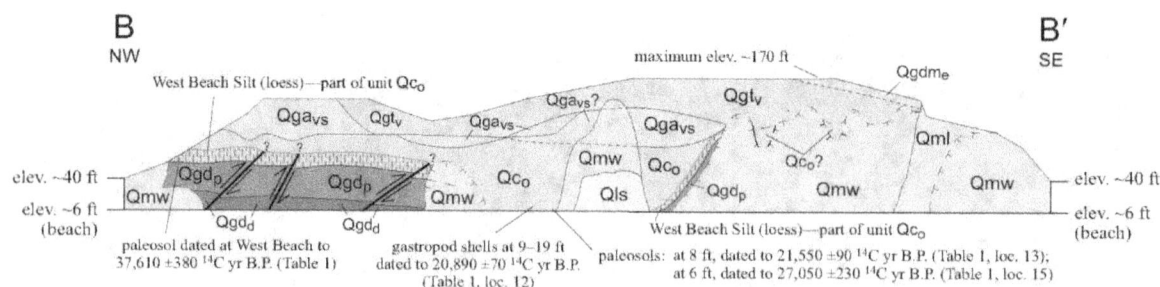

Figure 8. Schematic northwest—southeast geologic cross-section along the bluff from Ebey's Landing to Fort Casey, Ebey's Landing National Historical Reserve, illustrating abundant mass-wasting (Qmw) and landslide deposits (Qls) resulting from erosion. Erosion may also destroy cultural sites. The Double Bluff Drift [Qgd(d)] is the oldest unit exposed in the reserve. Black lines with arrows represent faults, with the arrows indicating the direction of movement. Vertical exaggeration is 10 times. The schematic begins and ends at the 40-ft contour at the top of the bluff on the base map. Map units are the same as those found on the Map Unit Properties Table and the enclosed GIS map. The locations from which radiocarbon dates were obtained are reported on Table 1 of Polenz et al. (2005; Attachment 1). The location of the cross-section is also indicated on the Geologic Map Overview Graphic. Cross-section from Polenz et al. (2005).

Figure 9. Partially excavated log in the low intertidal zone at the northwestern end of Penn Cove. The log is in an upright position, and shells are attached to the bark. Photograph courtesy Michael Polenz (Washington Department of Natural Resources).

Blowers Bluff schematic section

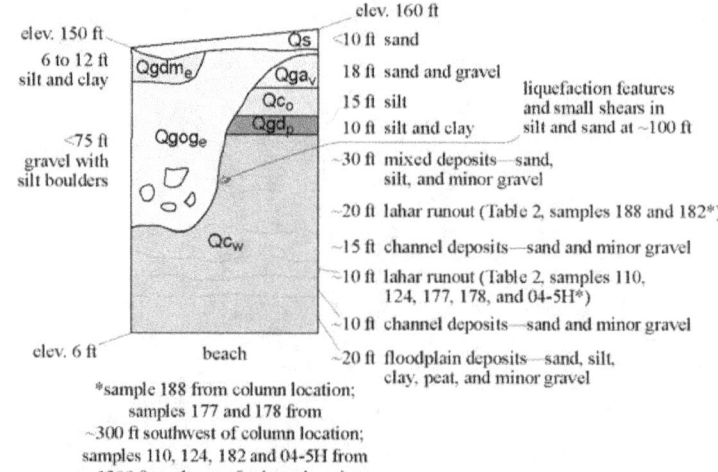

elev. 160 ft

elev. 150 ft

Qs — <10 ft sand

6 to 12 ft
silt and clay — Qgdm_e

Qga_v — 18 ft sand and gravel

Qc_o — 15 ft silt

liquefaction features
and small shears in
silt and sand at ~100 ft

Qgd_p — 10 ft silt and clay

<75 ft
gravel with
silt boulders — Qgog_e

~30 ft mixed deposits—sand,
silt, and minor gravel

~20 ft lahar runout (Table 2, samples 188 and 182*)

~15 ft channel deposits—sand and minor gravel

Qc_w — ~10 ft lahar runout (Table 2, samples 110,
124, 177, 178, and 04-5H*)

~10 ft channel deposits—sand and minor gravel

elev. 6 ft — beach

~20 ft floodplain deposits—sand, silt,
clay, peat, and minor gravel

*sample 188 from column location;
samples 177 and 178 from
~300 ft southwest of column location;
samples 110, 124, 182 and 04-5H from
~1200 ft northeast of column location

Figure 10. Blowers Bluff. Located 1.6 km (1 mi) east along the shore from the parking lot at Penn Cove County Park, Blowers Bluff exposes units from the Whidbey Formation [oldest, map unit Qc(w)] to late Pleistocene sand (youngest, map unit Qs). Human in lower left corner for scale. The accompanying schematic illustrates the stratigraphic order of the units and includes unit symbols and lithology. The "lahar runout" deposit contains pebbles from an eruption of Glacier Peak. High-energy gravel deposits [map unit Qgog(e)] filled channels that truncated older units and eroded down to the Whidbey Formation. Sample numbers are from Table 2 in Polenz (2005) and Polenz et al. (2005; Attachment 1). Photograph and schematic courtesy Michael Polenz (Washington Department of Natural Resources).

Geologic Features and Processes

This section describes the most prominent and distinctive geologic features and processes in Ebey's Landing National Historical Reserve.

The diverse physical and visual landscapes within the small geographic area of Ebey's Landing National Historical Reserve are closely tied to the primary purpose of the reserve, which is to preserve and protect the cultural landscape. The reserve contains excellent examples of both glacial and post-glacial features and processes. Together with the distinctive climate, rain shadow location, soils, and maritime influence, these geologic features have helped shape the historical landscape of Whidbey Island and the unusual diversity of plant and animal species, communities, and habitats (National Park Service 2006).

The Final General Management Plan and Environmental Impact Statement (National Park Service 2006) for Ebey's Landing National Historical Reserve has divided the reserve into ten Landscape Character Areas based on the significant landforms and critical landscape components defined by NPS Landscape Architect Cathy Gilbert (Gilbert 1985). This section first outlines the glacial and post-glacial geologic features in the reserve and then associates each of these features with the appropriate Landscape Character Area.

Glacial Features and Processes

Glacial sediments dominate most of the Puget Lowland, including Ebey's Landing National Historical Reserve. No bedrock exposures are present in the reserve. Rather, unconsolidated Pleistocene gravel, sand, silt, and clay deposits are exposed (fig. 4).

Deposits of the Double Bluff Glaciation

Deposited approximately 185,000–125,000 years ago, the Double Bluff Drift [map unit Qdg(d)], is the oldest unit in the reserve and is exposed for only about 560 m (1,500 ft) of shoreline southeast of Ebey's Landing (fig. 8). The unit consists of silt, clay, and diamicton deposited in a glaciomarine setting similar to the younger Vashon Till [map unit Qgt(v)]. A diamicton refers to poorly sorted, unconsolidated sediments with a wide variety of grain sizes enclosed within a sandy- to silty- or clayey- matrix.

Interglacial Deposits of the Whidbey Formation

In contrast to the glaciomarine sediments of the Double Bluff Drift, the sediments of the overlying Whidbey Formation [map unit Qc(w)] represent deposition during an interglacial period 125,000–80,000 years ago when the glaciers had melted and retreated to the north of Whidbey Island. More than 30 m (100 ft) of the Whidbey Formation forms the base of Blowers Bluff, which provides the most complete stratigraphic section within Ebey's Landing National Historical Reserve (fig. 10).

At Blowers Bluff, a vertical cliff face of up to 8 m (25 ft) of sand, silt, clay, and peat that were deposited in a floodplain form the base of the Whidbey Formation (fig. 10). These sediments are overlain by gravelly, cross-bedded channel sands that are interbedded with lahar deposits from Glacier Peak eruptions. The flat-lying deposits of sand, silt, peat, clay, and occasional gravel resemble the low-energy depositional setting of today's lower Skagit River floodplain and channel, which is located approximately 8–32 km (5–20 mi) northeast of the reserve (Polenz 2005; Polenz et al 2005). Peat and organic matter appear to be scarce in the upper part of the Whidbey Formation, above the channel sand deposits; this scarcity may reflect a climate shift that preceded renewed glaciation approximately 80,000 years ago (Polenz 2005).

Deposits of the Possession Glaciation

About 80,000–60,000 years ago, glaciers advanced again into the area. Glacial marine (glaciomarine) drift and underlying glacial till and outwash sand deposits of the Possession Drift [map unit Qgd(p)] were deposited in front of this glacial advance. The silt, clay, and diamicton of the glaciomarine drift are compact and commonly contain shells. The drift can be indistinguishable from the till, which is composed of ash-gray to white, compact, sandy diamicton. The outwash sand is medium- to fine-grained (Polenz et al. 2005).

Along Blowers Bluff, about 3 m (10 ft) of glaciomarine Possession Drift overlies the Whidbey Formation, but the unit thickens to the north (Polenz 2005). At West Beach and within 2.4 km (1.5 mi) southeast of Ebey's Landing, the unit is predominantly sand (Polenz et al. 2005).

Sediments of the Possession Drift are similar to those of the Vashon Till [map unit Qgt(v)] and Everson glaciomarine drift [map unit Qgom(e)]. Consequently, the Possession Drift can only be identified if local field relations indicate that the deposits are older than the Vashon Till. Surficial drift deposits are assumed to be associated with the younger deposits of the Fraser Glaciation (Polenz 2005).

Deposits of the Olympia Nonglacial Interval

Olympia nonglacial deposits [map unit Qc(o)] overly the Possession Drift and are similar to those in the Whidbey Formation. In many locations, the presence of Possession Drift sediments provides the only way to distinguish the silt, sand, and occasional interbeds of fine gravel comprising the Olympia nonglacial deposits from those of the Whidbey Formation (Polenz 2005).

At Blowers Bluff, the Olympia nonglacial deposits form a 4.6-m (15-ft)- thick section of homogeneous buff to light yellowish-brown silt (fig. 11). However, the interval can be as thick and lithologically diverse as the Whidbey Formation found at the base of the bluff (Polenz 2005).

The Olympia sediments at Blowers Bluff deserve a special note. The silt, known as West Beach silt, has been interpreted as a loess deposit (Polenz et al. 2005). Loess is wind-blown silt that is deposited near the margins of former or existing glaciers. Typically, compacted loess forms vertical bluffs, like those at Blowers Bluff. Eastern Washington contains widespread loess deposits, but with the exception of the West Beach silt, loess is surprisingly sparse in western Washington. The only recognized exposures of West Beach silt are located in the rain shadow area northeast of the Olympic Mountains. The paucity of loess in western Washington may be the result of the wet regional climate, but it is not clear whether the climate has caused a lack of deposition, lack of preservation, or both (Polenz 2005). Radiometric dates from overlying and underlying units constrain the age of the West Beach silt in the reserve area to between about 37,000 and 27,000 radiocarbon years B.P. (before present, used to express radiocarbon years before 1950; Polenz 2005).

Habitat requirements for the freshwater clams and snails found in the Olympia nonglacial sediments south of Ebey's Landing and along the north shore of Penn Cove favor freshwater, low-energy depositional environments similar to those evidenced in the Whidbey Formation. Dates obtained from shells and paleosols indicate that the Olympia nonglacial interval occurred approximately 37,000–16,800 years B.P. (Polenz 2005).

Deposits of the Vashon Stade

The last major glacial advance into the region occurred approximately 18,000–14,000 years ago and is known as the Vashon Stade of the Fraser Glaciation (Washington State Department of Natural Resources 2010). Roughly 1,200–1,300 m (3,900–4,300 ft) of ice blanketed Whidbey Island during this time. Sediments representing Vashon glacial deposits include outwash sand and gravel that was deposited in advance of the approaching ice [map unit Qga(vs)] and deposits of unsorted, boulder-clay layers referred to as Vashon Till [map unit Qgt(v)].

Although Vashon glacial deposits form the dominant landforms in many parts of the Puget Lowland, they are relatively sparse in Ebey's Landing National Historical Reserve. Rather, Everson Interstade recessional deposits dominate the landscape in the reserve. At Blowers Bluff, for example, the outwash sand and gravel layer is about 5.5 m (18 ft) thick, but it is truncated to the south and discontinuous to the north. Vashon Till is absent at Blowers Bluff, but the unit thickens to approximately 9 m (30 ft) farther north (Polenz 2005). However, the absence of Vashon glacial deposits at Blowers Bluff can be explained by the overlying unit and the processes responsible for its deposition.

On the south side of the Blowers Bluff exposure, a thick gravel unit has erased any evidence of Vashon glacial deposits and rests directly on the lower part of the Whidbey Formation. The gravel [map unit Qgog(e)] has also truncated all of the Vashon and pre-Vashon units that are exposed on the north side of Blowers Bluff. Along the Penn Cove shoreline, the high-energy gravel truncates at least 12 m (40 ft) of pre-Fraser units (fig. 10). The steeply- dipping, crudely to well-bedded gravel contains lenses of sand, silt, and clay, as well as boulders and clay rip-up clasts from the underlying units. The presence of boulders, rip-up clasts, and steeply- dipping beds, and the evidence of dynamic scouring of the underlying units, are indicators of a high-energy flow regime that eroded most of the Vashon glacial deposits as the glaciers receded to the north (Polenz 2005; Polenz et al. 2005).

South of Coupeville, low, smoothly rounded drumlins formed under the margin of the southward movement of ice during the Vashon Stade (fig. 6; Polenz et al. 2005). The long axes of these drumlins parallel this southward ice movement. Usually, a drumlin has a blunt nose in the direction of the ice approach and a gentler slope tapering in the other direction. The drumlins north of Coupeville have a similar north–south orientation that is overprinted by a southwest–trending alignment (fig. 6). This alignment may represent a reorientation of the ice flow to the southwest toward the end of the glaciation north of Coupeville.

Everson Interstade

Where contacts are exposed, high-energy gravel [map unit Qgog(e)] always stratigraphically underlies the Everson glaciomarine drift [map unit Qgdm(e)] and overlies the Vashon Till (Polenz 2005). A continuous sheet of gravel forms a gentle south-sloping topography north of Penn Cove, and the slope was formed by the erosion of older underlying units. Exposures at San de Fuca and in a gravel quarry 0.3 km (0.2 mi) south of the southwestern end of Penn Cove show the high-energy gravel unit grading into the Partridge Gravel [map unit Qgom(e); fig. 12]. The gradational contact between these two units suggests that the high-energy gravel is laterally equivalent to the Partridge Gravel and belongs to the Everson Interstade (Polenz 2005; Polenz et al. 2005).

The voluminous Partridge Gravel that forms the elevated terraces on either side of Ebey's Prairie probably came from the high-energy gravel at Blowers Bluff. The northern edge of the Partridge Gravel is known to have been in contact with the glacier. Consequently, the high-energy outwash deposit along the northern shore of Penn Cove likely represents a mostly or entirely subglacial flow deposit (Polenz 2005; Polenz et al. 2005).

The relatively thick Partridge Gravel forms the elevated landscape of Smith Prairie and the gentle topography west of Ebey's Prairie, south of Penn Cove. The Partridge Gravel represents a kame-delta complex in which outwash sand and gravel were deposited in a marine environment adjacent to the receding ice margin (Polenz

2005). Horizontal, sand-dominated bottom beds (bottom-set beds) reflect deposition on the sea floor. Low-energy gravity flow produced low-angle cross-bedding, flame structures, and other soft sediment deformation features in these bottom beds (fig. 13). Sloping beds of gravel and sand that formed at the front of an advancing delta overlie the bottom beds. These beds are known as foreset beds (fig. 14). As the delta built seaward, distributary channels formed on the top of the delta (top-set beds), transporting meltwater and outwash sand and gravel to the delta front (fig. 14; Polenz 2005: Polenz et al. 2005).

On average, the Partridge Gravel is 30–76 m- (100–250 ft) thick and contains approximately 0.8–2.5 km^3 (0.2–0.6 mi^3) of sand and gravel (Polenz et al. 2005). The coastal cliffs at Cedar Hollow expose 64 m (210 ft) of Partridge Gravel and 1.5–12 m (5–40 ft) of overlying post-glacial, wind-deposited, Holocene sand (map unit Qd; fig. 15). Foreset beds in the middle of the cliff grade down into bottom-set sand beds at the cliff base. The bottom-set beds contain occasional lenses of sand-sized fragments of volcanic rock, coal, peat, charred wood, and minor charcoal that were re-worked from older Whidbey Formation and Olympia nonglacial sediments (Polenz 2005). Top-set beds cap the kame-delta sequence.

Marine clams found in the top-set beds of the Partridge Gravel helped to prove that the unit was a marine sequence rather than a lake deposit, as previously interpreted (Carlstad 1992; Polenz 2005). The clams could also provide constraining radiocarbon dates for the break-up of the Vashon glacial ice and the subsequent incursion of marine water into the region that initiated the Everson Interstade (see the Geologic History section).

Cedar Hollow is one of many bowl-shaped depressions formed in Ebey's Landing National Historical Reserve (fig. 6). Called kettles because of their shape, these depressions formed when stagnant blocks of ice that had been buried by Partridge Gravel melted, allowing the overlying sand and gravel to collapse into the resulting subterranean void. On the margins of the closed depression, small shear planes formed in the Partridge Gravel (fig. 16). The collapse caused the top-set beds, which are normally horizontal, to curve down into the depression.

Many kettles of diverse sizes formed north and east of Cedar Hollow and some formed east of Coupeville (fig. 6). All of these kettles formed near the Everson Interstade ice margin that was located just south of Penn Cove, along the Coupeville moraine. Their spatial clustering confirms the deposition of the Partridge Gravel near the margin of the melting ice sheet (Polenz 2005).

At the time of the Partridge Gravel deposit approximately 14,000 years ago, a temporary ice margin existed at the northern end of Ebey's Prairie. The recognition of this ice margin is based on the 150–240 m- (500–800 ft)-wide, east–west trending, gentle ridge that extends across Coupeville. Known as the Coupeville moraine [map unit Qgim(e)], this ridge aligns with the northern limit of the Partridge Gravel, suggesting that it formed at the margin of the ice sheet. The blanket of glaciomarine drift that covers Ebey's Prairie may thicken to the south, which would also indicate that the moraine represents a temporary ice margin (Polenz 2005).

The moraine consists of cobbly to boulder, angular to rounded gravel in a loose, powdery matrix of finer-grained sediments (fig. 17). More erratic boulders litter the moraine's surface than anywhere else in Ebey's Landing National Historical Reserve (Polenz 2005; Polenz et al. 2005).

Both the high-energy gravel and Partridge Gravel grade upward into glaciomarine drift [map unit Qgdm(e)] that was deposited on the sea floor during the Everson Interstade (fig. 12). Thick glaciomarine drift covers Ebey's Prairie and is further evidence for a late glacial incursion of marine water into the region (Polenz et al. 2005). At the glacial maximum of the Vashon Stade, approximately 900–1,200 m (3,000–4,000 ft) of ice depressed the crust in the Puget Lowland (Polenz 2005). The ice prevented seawater from flooding the area, but once the ice melted, seawater filled Ebey's Prairie until the crust rebounded in response to the removal of its weight. The gentle mounds present on the surface of Ebey's Prairie, including the three hills southeast of Ebey's Landing, are drumlins that have had their original topographic profile subdued by the blanket of glaciomarine drift (Polenz 2005).

Some of the thickest deposits of glaciomarine drift are found at Ebey's Landing. The cliff consists of at least 12 m (40 ft) of glaciomarine drift overlain by 1.2–3 m (4–10 ft) of fine sand (map unit Qd). The sand, silt, and clay of the glaciomarine drift contain marine shells and a few dropstones (oversized rocks transported out to sea on floating pieces of ice). About 0.2 m (0.5 ft) of pebbly gravel forms a thin layer at the top of the glaciomarine drift. This layer has been interpreted as an emergent deposit, such as a beach deposit, that marks the end of marine inundation into the area (Domack 1983; Polenz 2005).

At Blowers Bluff, glaciomarine drift overlies high-energy gravel (fig. 10). As at Ebey's Landing, the unit contains boulders and clumps of till that were rafted into position on icebergs and then dropped to the bottom of the sea when the ice melted.

When the ice melted and the glaciers retreated approximately 13,000 years ago, the region remained depressed for a brief (in geologic time) period. Sea level rose and glaciomarine drift was deposited across the reserve area. However, once the thick ice sheet was removed, the land rebounded and Whidbey Island emerged above sea level. The landforms and deposits that today occupy central Whidbey Island have changed little in the last 10,000 years.

Post-glacial Features and Processes

Numerous post-glacial features have been mapped in Ebey's Landing National Historical Reserve, including beach and dune deposits, sheet sands, peat, marsh and lagoon deposits, mass-wasting and landslide deposits, and paleosols (ancient soils; Polenz et al. 2005). About 0.2 m (0.5 ft) to 1.2 m (4 ft) of late Pleistocene fine sand and silt (map unit Qs) blankets the reserve area and typically forms topsoil. The unit, however, has been mapped only where it appears to exceed 1.5 m (5 ft) in thickness (Polenz et al. 2005). At Blowers Bluff, 2.4–3 m (8–10 ft) of this post-glacial sand caps the stratigraphic sequence (fig. 10).

The sand sheet appears to have a mixed sedimentological origin. In places, such as Cedar Hollow, the well-rounded, well-sorted, well-drained sand appears to be eolian in origin. However, the angular grain morphology of the sand sheet about 0.5 km (0.3 mi) north of the Libby Road beach suggests a glaciomarine, diamicton source. Regardless of origin, however, this sand sheet has a greater degree of soil development and stratigraphically underlies the modern dunes (map unit Qd; Polenz 2005).

At Cedar Hollow, the late Pleistocene sand sheet is capped by a paleosol that lies below a fossil assemblage dated to approximately 10,000 years ago (see the Paleontological Resources section). This paleosol is absent in most places, where the sand sheet forms the uppermost geologic deposit and is part of the modern surface. However, the thick Holocene dunes separate the paleosol from the modern surface at Cedar Hollow (fig. 18; Polenz 2005).

The paleosol separating the late Pleistocene sand sheet from modern dune sand is the most strongly developed paleosol in the Cedar Hollow section. Significantly, such a strong soil profile requires sufficient time to develop without input from wind-blown sand. Details about this time period are scarce, but the soil developed either during a period of environmental stability or in a paleoenvironment that was more conducive to soil development than the previous and subsequent environments (Carlstad 1992; Polenz 2005). Further study of the paleosol may provide insight into the evolution of the Puget Lowland climate and ecosystem since the last glaciation (Polenz 2005).

Hills and ridges of wind-blown sand dunes (map unit Qd) have formed on upland surfaces and in kettle sidewalls along or near west-facing bluffs north of Ebey's Landing. The sand is moderately to well sorted, and dune morphology suggests that its depositional environment lacked the forests that cover most of these dunes today. Limited soil development on the dunes and their location within 0.8 km (0.5 mi) of the present day shoreline bluffs, however, suggest that deposition may also be recent and ongoing (Polenz et al. 2005). The coastal cliffs at Cedar Hollow expose 1.5–12 m (5–40 ft) of post-glacial, wind-deposited sand (fig. 15). The sand has yielded numerous mammal and bird bone fossils (see the Paleontological Resources section).

Peat deposits (map unit Qp) include organic-rich mineral sediments deposited in closed depressions. The peat, muck, silt, and clay associated with wetlands are the freshwater equivalents of the organic-rich marsh sediments (map unit Qm) deposited in saltwater or brackish marsh (estuarine or lagoonal) environments. Peat deposits may grade downward into marsh deposits.

Grasser's Lagoon is a 7.7-ha (19-ac) salt marsh that is tidally inundated twice daily. The relationship between geology and ecosystem management is illustrated by the rocky sandspit that forms the outer boundary of the lagoon. The spit supports significant numbers of shore-birds including high concentrations of turnstones, surfbirds, and rock sandpipers.

A 30–45-m- (100–150-ft-) wide beach consisting of sand, gravel, and cobbles separates Perego's Lagoon from the inlet. This coastal lagoon is located south of Point Partridge and north of Ebey's Landing. Longshore currents deposit eroded upland sediments along this stretch of coast, which also is impacted by moderate wave action. The cliff face bordering the lake rises approximately 73 m (240 ft) from the water's edge.

Crockett Lake, the largest inland water feature on the reserve, was originally a salt marsh opening to Admiralty Bay (National Park Service 2006). The lake has been severely altered by early settlers and local residents. Tidal gates were installed in 1948, and lake levels have been manipulated since then, diminishing the productivity and scenic value of Crockett Lake. The tidal gates are still in place but in disrepair. It is unclear to what extent the gates continue to inhibit natural water flow, sediment flux, and fish passage.

Beach deposits (map unit Qb) contain primarily sand and cobbles but may include boulders, silt, pebbles, and clay. The deposits consist of well-sorted mixtures of sediment derived locally from shoreline bluffs, underlying materials, and sediment carried in by longshore drift.

Mass-wasting (map unit Qmw) and landslide deposits (map unit Qls) are generally unsorted and are located at the base of unstable, or potentially unstable, slopes (fig. 8). Many of these deposits are too small to map at a 1:24,000 scale, but all shoreline bluffs in the reserve are subject to episodic landsliding. Most slide deposits are removed by beach wave action (Polenz et al. 2005).

Paleontological Resources

Pleistocene and Holocene fossils have been discovered in Ebey's Landing National Historical Reserve and offer opportunities for education, interpretation, and future scientific research in the park (Fay et al. 2009). In 2004, Pleistocene-aged Olympia nonglacial deposits [map unit Qc(o)] yielded a mastodon (proboscidean) tusk (fig. 19; Michael Polenz, Geologist, Washington Department of Natural Resources, written communication, March 2011). When discovered, the tusk was quite weathered and has since been destroyed by erosion.

Radiocarbon ages from freshwater mollusks collected from this unit range from approximately 11,850 to 13,230 years B.P. (Polenz et al. 2005). Pollen collected from the Olympia nonglacial deposits in the Puget Lowland indicate that the cold, unstable climate dominating the region more than 48,000 years ago changed to a cool, moist climate approximately 33,000 years ago. At the end of the nonglacial interval and the beginning of Fraser Glaciation, cooler, dryer conditions prevailed (Hebda et al. 2007). Mammoth teeth, diatomites, pine cones, needles, branches, leaf prints, and in-situ tree roots discovered in these Olympia beds represent a diverse paleoecosystem during this time (Troost 2002).

Pleistocene glaciomarine drift from the Everson Interstade [map unit Qgdm(e)] contains marine shells. One of these shells, collected north of the reserve, recorded a radiocarbon age of 13,650 years B.P. (Polenz et al. 2005).

Pleistocene and Holocene post-glacial deposits have yielded a variety of animal and plant fossils (Fay et al. 2009). The upright tree trunk (fig. 9) discovered in the estuary at the northwestern end of Penn Cove provided evidence for tectonic subsidence prior to 1850 C.E. (Polenz 2005).

A concentrated bed of disarticulated skeletal remains from a variety of taxa was discovered in dune sands (map unit Qd) (fig. 20). The fossil land snails, birds, and mammals from this site have provided significant clues about the paleoenvironment of the area about 10,000 years ago (Mustoe and Carlstadt 1995; Polenz 2005; Fay et al. 2009). This site in Ebey's Landing National Historical Reserve contains the only known record of early Holocene, terrestrial animals in the Pacific Northwest, and documents the transition from late Pleistocene to more modern Holocene fauna (Mustoe et al. 2005; Fay et al. 2009).

Other geologic units in Ebey's Landing National Historical Reserve also may contain fossils. The Double Bluff Drift [map unit Qgd(d)], for example, was deposited at a time when large animals flourished in the region. Although no fossils have been discovered in the Whidbey Formation [map unit Qc(w)] within Ebey's Landing National Historical Reserve, mammoth tusks, teeth, and bones are documented from the unit's type

section, located 25 km (15 mi) southeast of the reserve at West Useless Bay, Whidbey Island (Easterbrook et al. 1967, 2003).

The Possession Drift [map unit Qgd(p)] contains shells, but their variety, quality, and distribution have not been described (Polenz et al. 2005; Fay et al. 2009). In British Columbia, outwash deposits of the Vashon Stade of the Fraser Glaciation contain mammoth remains, but no fossils have been found in this unit [map units Qga(v), Qga(vs)] within Ebey's Landing National Historical Reserve (Fay et al. 2009).

A more detailed summary of the paleontological resources of Ebey's Landing National Historical Reserve, as well as recommendations for paleontological resource management, may be found in Fay et al. (2009).

Landscape Character Areas

Table 1 summarizes some of the geological features associated with the Landscape Character Areas defined by Gilbert (1985).

These landscape areas connect the geology with the reserve's cultural history. Similar to today's farmers, for example, American Indians in the past grew crops on the relatively flat topography and rich soil of Ebey's Prairie. Deposition of the clay-rich glaciomarine sediments [map unit Qgdm(e)] subdued the topography, retained moisture, and provided the parent material for soil development.

The Partridge Gravel [map unit Qgom(e)] rendered Smith Prairie an attractive site for the Coupeville airport. The thick deposits of outwash channel sand and gravel are responsible for the well-drained, elevated, and flat landscape of Smith Prairie.

Penn Cove also originated through geologic processes. Swift-flowing rivers from pressurized subglacial meltwater carved a trough into the sediments between Coupeville and the uplands to the north, and this trough became Penn Cove (Michael Polenz, Geologist, Washington Department of Natural Resources, written communication, March 2011). The cove offers an ideal site for the cultivation of mussels and provides a naturally sheltered harbor for the town.

Figure 11. The Olympia nonglacial interval exposed at the top of Blowers Bluff consists of about 4.6 m (15 ft) of homogeneous West Beach silt (part of geologic map unit Qc(o). A pebbly paleosol (ancient soil layer; arrow) lies at the base of the silt. The gravelly Possession Drift, which includes some erratic boulders, forms the cliff beneath the paleosol and West Beach silt. Photograph courtesy Michael Polenz (Washington Department of Natural Resources).

Figure 12. Relationship between high-energy gravel [map unit Qgog(e)], Partridge Gravel [map unit Qgom(e)], and glaciomarine drift [map unit Qgdm(e)]. In this gravel quarry, located 0.3 km (0.2 mi) south of the southwestern end of Penn Cover, the large-scale channel cross-bedding in the Partridge Gravel overlies the high-energy, glacial gravel that is exposed at Blowers Bluff and at the northern to western periphery of Penn Cove. The arrows indicate the base of two of these channels with a younger channel truncating an older channel. Cross-beds form as sediment (in this case, gravel) is deposited parallel to the channel boundaries. In this quarry, the high-energy gravel is covered by debris at the base of the Partridge Gravel. Large silt boulders in the gravel become increasingly common in the lower levels of the unit. Glaciomarine drift covers the Partridge Gravel. Where the Partridge Gravel is missing, glaciomarine drift overlies the high-energy gravel. Photograph courtesy Michael Polenz (Washington Department of Natural Resources).

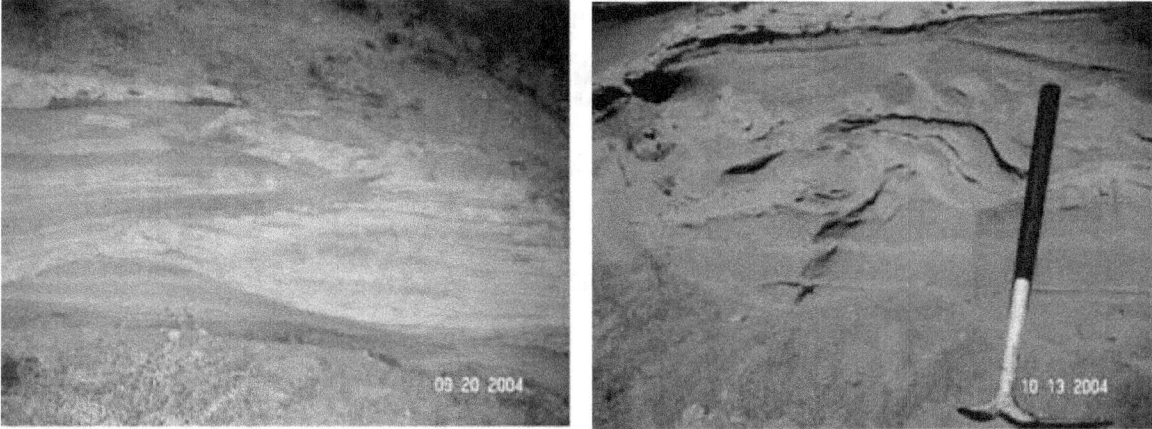

Figure 13. Sedimentary features in the bottom-set beds of Partridge Gravel. Left: Low-energy currents formed wavy cross-beds in fine sand to silt deposited on the sea floor. These beds are now exposed at beach level along shoreline bluffs 0.8 km (0.5 mi) northeast of the Ebey's Landing beach access parking lot. Right: Flame structures (features that resemble flames) formed in more proximal, coarser bottom-set sand beds of the Partridge Gravel. This exposure is also at beach level, and is located approximately 2.4 km (1.5 mi) northwest of the exposure depicted in the left panel. Photographs courtesy Michael Polenz (Washington Department of Natural Resources).

Figure 14. Kame-delta top-set and foreset sand and gravel beds in the Partridge Gravel. The top-set beds are horizontal and overlie the gently-dipping foreset beds. Channel sand and gravel deposited in the top-set beds represent shallower depositional environments than do the foreset beds, which formed at the front of a delta. As the delta built seaward, the marine environment became more shallow and top-set beds prograded over foreset beds. View is to the southeast of the southern quarry wall at Smith Prairie, southeast of Coupeville. The slope of the foreset beds records a southwesterly paleoflow during the deposition of the Partridge Gravel at Smith Prairie. Photograph courtesy Michael Polenz (Washington Department of Natural Resources).

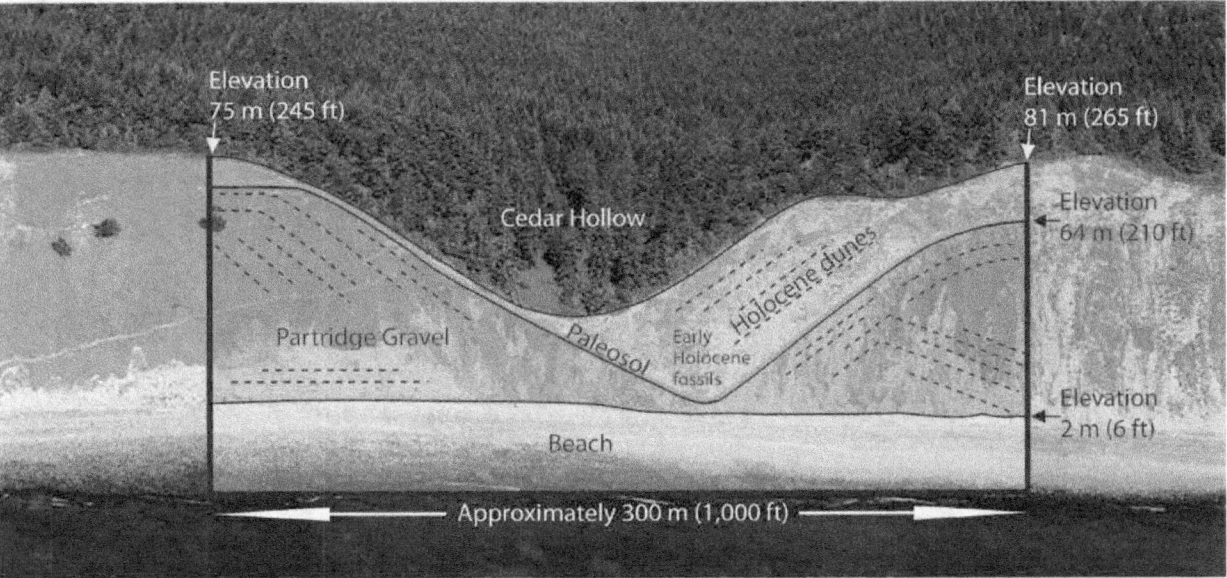

Figure 15. Northwest-trending shoreline at Cedar Hollow showing the bottom-set, foreset, and top-set beds of the Partridge Gravel [map unit Qgom(e)] and younger, eolian sand (map unit Qd) that blew into the depression to cover the Partridge Gravel. A paleosol formed on the surface of the Partridge Gravel prior to the deposition of the wind-blown sand. The upper image is the same as the lower image with explanatory schematic. View is to the northeast. Photograph courtesy of the Washington State Department of Ecology and extracted from Polenz (2005). Annotation by Trista Thornberry-Ehrlich after Polenz (2005).

Figure 16. Shear planes in the Partridge Gravel. These features document the deformation of Partridge Gravel strata during the formation of Cedar Hollow. View is to the northeast. The arrow points to one of the northwest-dipping shear planes. Hammer for scale. Photograph courtesy Michael Polenz (Washington Department of Natural Resources).

Figure 17. Coupeville moraine exposed in a road cut along Broadway Street in Coupeville. The variety of clast sizes indicates that the unit is poorly sorted. The clasts range from angular (suggesting that they did not travel far from their origin) to well-rounded spheroids (suggesting the rounding of their edges during transport from their place of origin, usually implying a considerable transport distance). The unit also lacks sedimentary structures, such as cross-bedding or graded bedding. Hammer for scale. Photograph courtesy (Michael Polenz, Washington Department of Natural Resources).

Figure 18. Paleosol beneath the Holocene dune sand (map unit Qd) in Cedar Hollow. This paleosol (red-brown layer) is more strongly developed than any other paleosol in the overlying sand. Hammer for scale. Photograph courtesy Michael Polenz (Washington Department of Natural Resources).

Figure 19. Mastodon tusk. In 2004, a poorly preserved portion of a mastodon tusk (above the hammer head) was exposed in Olympia nonglacial deposits [Qc(o)] along the cliff between Ebey's Landing and Admiralty Head. The fossil has since been removed by erosion. Photograph courtesy Michael Polenz (Washington Department of Natural Resources).

 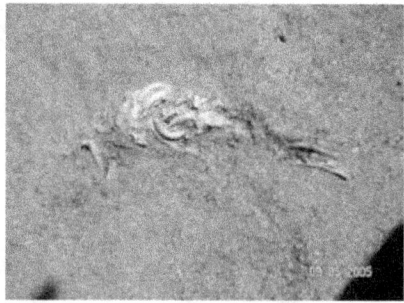 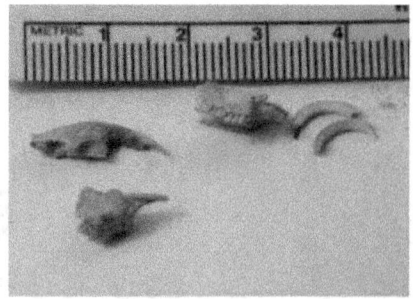

Figure 20. Fossil fragments from dune sand (Qd), Ebey's Landing National Historical Reserve. Left: Fossil fragments in the dune sand. Center: Close-up of one rodent fossil exposure. Right: Some of the microtine rodent (vole) bone and tooth remains that have been radiometrically dated to 9,420 to 9,130 years of age (Polenz 2005). Photographs courtesy Michael Polenz (Washington Department of Natural Resources).

Table 1. Landscape Character Areas and Geologic Features.

Landscape Character Area	Physical Description	Geologic Features
San de Fuca Uplands	Gently rolling hills that begin at the shoreline of Penn Cove and slope onto agricultural land.	Gently rolling hills of Vashon Till.
Penn Cove	Nearshore and shoreline habitats in mudflat tidelands, high sandy bluffs, beaches, and eelgrass beds.	Beaches; mudflats; high, unstable sandy bluffs.
West Coastal Strip	A 13-km (8-mi) strip of narrow sand and rocky beaches forming the western boundary of the reserve adjacent to Admiralty Inlet and the Strait of Juan de Fuca.	Narrow sand and rocky beaches; steep, unstable bluffs; ravines.
Kettle and Pratt Woodlands (West Woodlands)	Dense forests with kettles (glacial features) and trails that connect to Fort Ebey State Park.	Kettles up to 61 m (200 ft) deep; Lake Pondilla.
Coupeville	The commercial center of the reserve and Washington State's second oldest town.	Built mainly on glaciomarine drift (clay and silt).
Ebey's Prairie	The largest natural prairie on Whidbey Island, located in the central portion of the reserve.	Blanket of glaciomarine sediments have smoothed out the underlying, gently rolling hills of Vashon Till.
Fort Casey Uplands	Gently rolling hills bearing forest, fields, and residential areas.	Gently rolling hills of Vashon Till.
Crockett Prairie	Natural, open prairie adjacent to Crockett Lake, Keystone Spit, and Admiralty Bay.	Crockett Lake and prairie floored by glaciomarine drift.
Parker and Patmore Woodlands	Densely wooded second- and third-growth Douglas fir forest located along a ridge in the eastern portion of the reserve.	Ridge of Partridge Gravel.
Smith Prairie	A 240-ha (600-ac) natural prairie surrounded by Douglas fir forest.	Prairie underlain by Partridge Gravel.

Compiled from Gilbert (1985).

Geologic History

This section describes the rocks and unconsolidated deposits that appear on the digital geologic map of Ebey's Landing National Historical Reserve, the environment in which those units were deposited, and the timing of geologic events that formed the present landscape.

Whidbey Island, nearby islands, and peninsulas are relatively young, Quaternary geomorphic features that emerged from the Salish Sea (the marine equivalent of the Puget Lowland) after the most recent ice age glacial retreat (fig. 21). The metamorphic, structural, and depositional history of the buried bedrock core of these islands, however, is exceptionally complex, and its origin remains a subject of debate (Michael Polenz, Geologist, Washington Department of Natural Resources, written communication, March 2011). Pre-Devonian and Devonian (416–359 million years ago) limestone, argillite, black shale, siltstone, and andesitic tuff are the oldest rocks in the islands, but these rocks, like the overlying Pennsylvanian and Permian submarine volcanic rocks, originally formed in paleo-environments that were far removed from the western margin of North America.

During the Jurassic (200–145 million years ago), islands and oceanic material of a foreign terrane known as Wrangellia began to be accreted to the North American continent (fig. 22). Significant accretion continued during the Late Cretaceous (100–66 million years ago), but the relationship between these accreted terrains and Whidbey Island is not well understood.

While these older rocks form the foundation beneath the San Juan Islands, the present landforms and island geometry are the result of Pleistocene glaciers. During the late Pleistocene Fraser and earlier glaciations, the Cordilleran Ice Sheet extended from the mountains of coastal southern and southeastern Alaska, along the Coast Mountains of British Columbia, and into northern Washington and northwestern Montana (fig. 23). This ice sheet was the smaller of two great continental ice sheets that covered North America during the Quaternary. At times, the Cordilleran Ice Sheet likely coalesced with the western margin of the larger Laurentide Ice Sheet to form a continuous ice sheet over 4,000 km (2,500 mi) wide (Booth et al. 2004).

The oldest Pleistocene sediments exposed on Whidbey Island, those of the Double Bluff Drift [map unit Qgd(d)], are found at beach level south of Ebey's Landing and were deposited approximately 185,000–125,000 years B.P. (fig. 8). The Double Bluff silt, clay, and diamicton were deposited in a marine environment that formed in front of an advancing ice sheet (Polenz et al. 2005). Older Pleistocene sediments may be exposed elsewhere on the island, but their presence and age have not yet been documented (Michael Polenz, Geologist, Washington Department of Natural Resources, written communication, March 2011).

The Whidbey Formation represents a warm, interglacial period that existed from about 125,000–80,000 years B.P. (Heusser and Heusser 1981; Polenz et al. 2005). Whidbey sediments were deposited in low-energy floodplains and deltas, such as the floodplain associated with the ancestral Skagit River. During the deposition of the Whidbey Formation, the ancestral Skagit (or possibly Stillaguamish) River flowed into the present Whidbey Island, suggesting that Skagit Bay did not exist and even the Saratoga Passage may have been absent (Polenz 2005).

Glaciers returned to the area approximately 80,000 years B.P. and remained until 60,000 years B.P. Streams flowing from the advancing glaciers deposited outwash sand, which was subsequently covered by the glacial till and glaciomarine clay and silt of the Possession Drift [map unit Qgd(p)].

In another interglacial period from 60,000–20,000 years B.P. the silt, clay, sand, and gravel of the Olympia nonglacial interval [map unit Qc(o)] were deposited in the Puget Lowland. These sediments are similar to those of the Whidbey Formation and were probably deposited in similar low-energy, freshwater paleoenvironments. Freshwater habitats are required for the clams and snails found in the Olympia nonglacial sediments south of Ebey's Landing, and for the mollusks found in similar sediments along the northern shore of Penn Cove (Polenz et al. 2005). The carbon-13 to carbon-12 ratios of the shells also suggest a freshwater setting.

About 18,000 years ago, the Puget Lobe of the Cordilleran ice sheet advanced from British Columbia to just south of Olympia, covering the entire Puget Lowland with glacial ice in the last major ice advance called the Fraser Glaciation (Washington State Department of Natural Resources 2010). The part of the Fraser Glaciation during which Cordilleran ice covered the Puget Lowland is called the Vashon Stade, and it is largely responsible for the present-day geomorphic features in the Puget Lowland. High-energy meltwater streams flowed from the front of the advancing glacier and deposited well-sorted sand and gravel over the region. The thickness of the Vashon Stade ice reached approximately 1,200–1,300 m (3,900–4,300 ft) on central Whidbey Island (Polenz et al. 2005).

Similar to previous glaciations, the Cordilleran ice sheet dammed the streams and rivers draining the Cascade Mountains. Flow was diverted south along the flanks of the Cascades and then around the terminus of the ice sheet south of Olympia. Finally, the waters flowed out the Chehalis River Valley to the Pacific Ocean. Drumlin orientation on Whidbey Island indicates that ice flow was mostly confined to a north-south direction.

As the ice thinned near the end of the Vashon Stade, recessional outwash sands and gravels covered large areas south of Seattle. These deposits are an important source of raw materials for concrete and other construction uses (Washington State Department of Natural Resources 2010). Late in the glaciation, a local ice front stabilized at Coupeville and remained long enough to allow the deposition of the Partridge Gravel [map unit Qgom(e)]. Sediments in the Partridge Gravel represent marine and kame-delta depositional environments, and exemplify the development of some of the best sand and gravel deposits (Polenz et al. 2005; Michael Polenz, Geologist, Washington Department of Natural Resources, written communication, March 2011).

Marine shells discovered in the Partridge Gravel at Cedar Hollow in Ebey's Landing National Historical Reserve may provide the oldest constraining radiocarbon dates for the breakup of the Vashon glacial ice and the beginning of the Everson Interstade (Carlstad 1992; Polenz 2005). To date, a marine shell found at Oak Harbor, a few kilometers north of the reserve, has yielded the oldest estimated date (13,650 B.P.) for the Everson Interstade. However, ice must have covered Oak Harbor and an ice front must have been present in Penn Cove when the Partridge Gravel was deposited. If an ice front had not been located in Penn Cove, then the outwash would have filled Penn Cove rather than forming the large delta terraces found east and west of Ebey's Prairie. If an isolated block of stagnant ice had occupied Penn Cove, then melting ice would not have provided enough meltwater and sediment to produce the Partridge Gravel. Rather, seawater must have flooded the ice-free areas south and west of Penn Cove while Oak Harbor remained covered by ice. Therefore, marine shells found at Cedar Hollow would be older than those at Oak Harbor (Polenz 2005; Polenz et al. 2005).

As the Vashon Stade ice retreated, seawater may have flowed under the thinning ice front, lifting the ice and causing it to break apart into ice bergs over much of the region. The overprint of southwest drumlinization north of the Coupeville moraine suggests that the ice collapse across Admiralty Inlet removed the confining pressure in the central to northern Puget Lowland and triggered a reorientation of the ice flow to a southwestern direction.

During the Everson Interstade, local sea level rose 66–70 m (216–229 ft). Glaciomarine drift deposits south of Lovejoy Point are about 67 m (220 ft) above present sea level. The Everson Interstade ended when post-glacial crustal rebound exceeded global sea level rise, causing the land in the reserve area to emerge. Evidence from a glaciomarine deposit 3 m (10 ft) above sea level along the northern shore of Penn Cove suggests an age of 12,690 years B.P. for the end of the Everson Interstade, thus suggesting that glaciation effectively ended in the reserve area somewhat earlier than 10,000 years B.P. (Polenz et al. 2005).

The fossil assemblage in the dune sand (map unit Qd) above the paleosol at Cedar Hollow suggests that the paleoenvironment was warmer and drier approximately 10,000 years B.P. than it is today (Mustoe et al. 2005; Polenz 2005). Further study of the paleosol beneath the dune sand may provide additional information regarding the paleoenvironment and paleoclimate at the end of the Everson Interstade.

Except for dune development and bluff formation due to coastal erosion, the landforms and deposits in Ebey's Landing National Historical Reserve have changed little since the end of the Everson Interstade. Dune development probably began about 10,000 years ago and continues along the western shore. Shoreline erosion began when sea level approximated modern sea level in the mid-Holocene.

The western coast of Washington continues to be an active plate tectonic zone, where the oceanic Juan de Fuca plate moves northeast and subducts beneath the North American plate at a rate of about 4 cm (1.6 in) per year (Booth et al. 2004). Seismographs record more than 1,000 earthquakes each year due to plate subduction. The Puget Lowland is classified as a Seismic Risk Zone 3 on a scale of 0 to 4, with 4 being the highest risk (Washington State Department of Natural Resources 2010). In 1949 and 2001, the epicenters of damaging earthquakes with Richter scale magnitudes of 7.1 and 6.8, respectively, were centered under Olympia, and the 1965 magnitude 6.5 earthquake was centered under Seattle/Tacoma. The most recent fault movement associated with documented surface rupture in the Whidbey Island area occurred between 1550 and 1850 C.E. (Polenz et al. 2005).

Eon	Era	Period	Epoch	Ma	Life Forms	North American Events
Phanerozoic	Cenozoic	Quaternary	Holocene	0.01	Modern humans	Cascade volcanoes (W)
			Pleistocene		Extinction of large mammals and birds	Worldwide glaciation
		Tertiary — Neogene	Pliocene	2.6	Large carnivores	Sierra Nevada Mountains (W)
			Miocene	5.3	Whales and apes	Linking of North and South America
		Tertiary — Paleogene	Oligocene	23.0		Basin-and-Range extension (W)
			Eocene	33.9		
			Paleocene	55.8	Early primates	Laramide Orogeny ends (W)
	Mesozoic	Cretaceous		65.5	Mass extinction / Placental mammals / Early flowering plants	Laramide Orogeny (W) / Sevier Orogeny (W) / Nevadan Orogeny (W)
		Jurassic		145.5	First mammals / Mass extinction	Elko Orogeny (W)
		Triassic		199.6	Flying reptiles / First dinosaurs	Breakup of Pangaea begins / Sonoma Orogeny (W)
	Paleozoic	Permian		251	Mass extinction / Coal-forming forests diminish	Supercontinent Pangaea intact / Ouachita Orogeny (S) / Alleghanian (Appalachian) Orogeny (E)
		Pennsylvanian		299	Coal-forming swamps / Sharks abundant / Variety of insects	Ancestral Rocky Mountains (W)
		Mississippian		318.1	First amphibians	
		Devonian		359.2	First reptiles / Mass extinction / First forests (evergreens)	Antler Orogeny (W) / Acadian Orogeny (E-NE)
		Silurian		416	First land plants	
		Ordovician		443.7	Mass extinction / First primitive fish / Trilobite maximum / Rise of corals	Taconic Orogeny (E-NE)
		Cambrian		488.3	Early shelled organisms	Avalonian Orogeny (NE) / Extensive oceans cover most of proto-North America (Laurentia)
				542		
	Proterozoic	Precambrian		2500	First multicelled organisms / Jellyfish fossil (670 Ma)	Supercontinent rifted apart / Formation of early supercontinent / Grenville Orogeny (E) / First iron deposits / Abundant carbonate rocks
	Archean			≈4000	Early bacteria and algae	Oldest known Earth rocks (≈3.96 billion years ago)
	Hadean				Origin of life?	Oldest moon rocks (4–4.6 billion years ago) / Formation of Earth's crust
				4600	Formation of the Earth	

Age of Mammals; Age of Dinosaurs; Age of Amphibians; Fishes; Marine Invertebrates

Figure 21. Geologic timescale. Included are major life history and tectonic events occurring on the North American continent. Red lines indicate major unconformities between eras. Radiometric ages shown are in millions of years (Ma). Compass directions in parentheses indicate the regional location of individual geologic events. Drafted by Trista Thornberry-Ehrlich (Colorado State University) using data from the U.S. Geological Survey (http://pubs.usgs.gov/fs/2007/3015/) and the International Commission on Stratigraphy (http://www.stratigraphy.org/view.php?id=25).

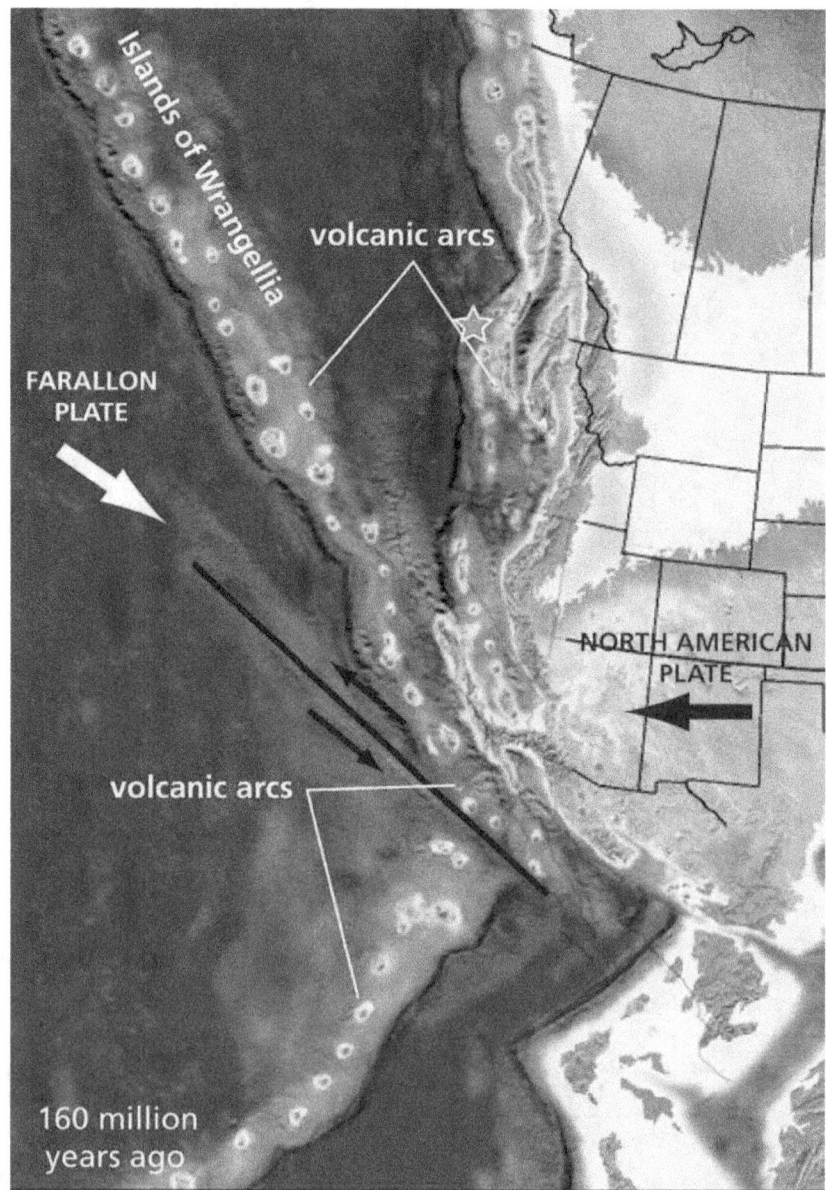

Figure 22. Middle Jurassic paleogeographic map of western North America. Approximately 160 million years ago, the islands of Wrangellia began to be accreted to the North American continent. Oblique convergence between the North American and the Farallon plates created a transform (strike-slip) fault along the southwestern margin of North America. Volcanic islands (volcanic arcs) formed above subduction zones. White arrows indicate the general direction of plate movement. Black arrows indicate movement along the transform fault. The yellow star represents the approximate location of today's Ebey's Landing National Historical Reserve. Brown colors represent land surface. Relative depths of marine water are divided into shallow (light blue) and deep (dark blue). Base map by Ron Blakey, Colorado Plateau Geosystems, Inc., http://cpgeosystems.com/jur160seattle.html, accessed September 19, 2011. Annotation by the author.

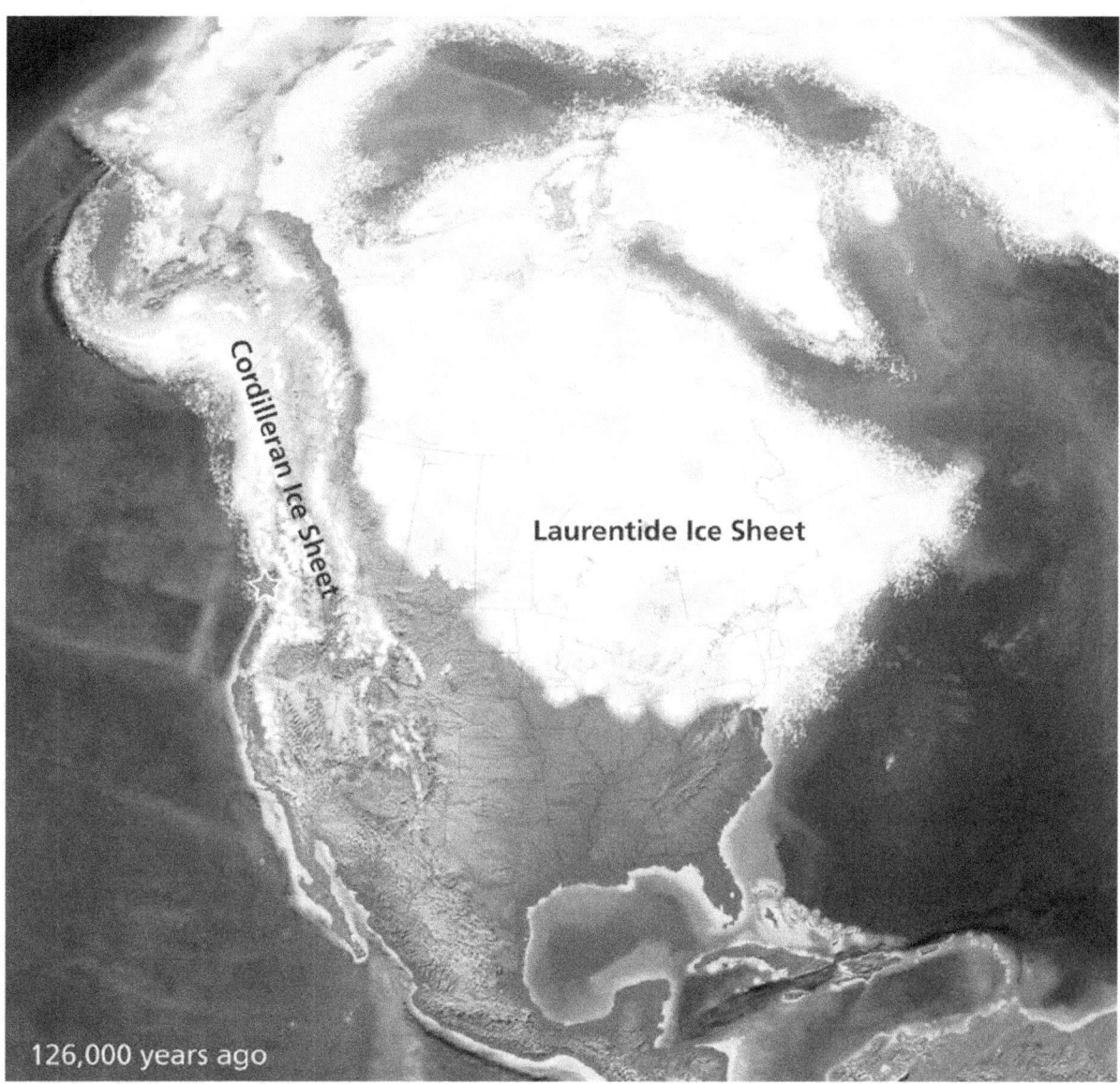

Figure 23. Pleistocene paleogeographic map of North America during a Pleistocene Ice Age. Approximately 126,000 years ago, the area of today's Ebey's Landing National Historical Reserve (yellow star) was covered by the Cordilleran Ice Sheet. Base map by Ron Blakey, Colorado Plateau Geosystems, Inc., http://cpgeosystems.com/namQ.jpg, accessed September 19, 2011. Annotation by the author.

Geologic Map Data

This section summarizes the geologic map data available for Ebey's Landing National Historical Reserve. It includes a fold-out geologic map overview and a summary table that lists each map unit displayed on the digital geologic map for the park. Complete GIS data are included on the accompanying CD and are also available at the Geologic Resources Inventory (GRI) publications website: (http://www.nature.nps.gov/geology/inventory/gre_publications.cfm).

Geologic Maps

Geologic maps facilitate an understanding of an area's geologic framework and the evolution of its present landscape. Using designated colors and symbols, geologic maps portray the spatial distribution and relationships of rocks and unconsolidated deposits. Geologic maps also may show geomorphic features, structural interpretations, and locations of past geologic hazards that may be prone to future activity. Additionally, anthropogenic features such as mines and quarries may be indicated on geologic maps.

Source Maps

The Geologic Resources Inventory (GRI) team converts digital and/or paper source maps into the GIS formats that conform to the GRI GIS data model. The GRI digital geologic map product also includes essential elements of the source maps including unit descriptions, map legend, map notes, references, and figures. The GRI team used the following source maps to create the digital geologic data for Ebey's Landing National Historical Reserve:

Polenz, M., S.L. Slaughter, J.D. Dragovich, and G.W. Thorsen. 2005. Geologic map of the Ebey's Landing National Historical Reserve, Island County, Washington. Washington Division of Geology and Earth Resources: Open-File Report 2005-2 (scale 1:24,000).

These source maps provided information for the "Geologic Issues," "Geologic Features and Processes," and "Geologic History" sections of this report.

Geologic GIS Data

The GRI team implements a GIS data model that standardizes map deliverables. The data model is included on the enclosed CD and is also available online (http://science.nature.nps.gov/im/inventory/geology /GeologyGISDataModel.cfm). This data model dictates GIS data structure including layer architecture, feature attribution, and relationships within ESRI ArcGIS software. The GRI team digitized the data for Ebey's Landing National Historical Reserve using data model version 2.1.

GRI digital geologic data for Ebey's Landing National Historical Reserve are included on the attached CD and are available through the NPS Natural Resource Information Portal (https://nrinfo.nps.gov/ Reference.mvc/Search). Enter "GRI" as the search text and select Ebey's Landing National Historical Reserve from the unit list. The following components and geology data layers are part of the data set:

- Data in ESRI geodatabase and shapefile GIS formats
- Layer files with feature symbology
- Federal Geographic Data Committee (FGDC)– compliant metadata
- An ancillary map information document (PDF) that contains all of the ancillary map information and graphics, including geologic unit correlation tables and map unit descriptions, legends, and other information captured from source maps.
- An ESRI map document file (.mxd) that displays the digital geologic data

Table 2. Geology data layers in the Ebey's Landing National Historical Reserve GIS data.

Data Layer	Code	On Geologic Map Overview?
Geologic Cross Section Lines	EBLASEC	Yes
Geologic Attitude Observation Localities	EBLAATD	No
Geologic Observation Localities	EBLAGOL	No
Geologic Sample Localities	EBLAGSL	No
Mine Point Features	EBLAMIN	No
Hazard Feature Lines	EBLAHZL	Yes
Geologic Line Features	EBLAGLF	Yes
Faults	EBLAFLT	Yes
Linear Geologic Units	EBLAGLN	Yes
Geologic Contacts	EBLAGLGA	Yes
Geologic Units	EBLAGLG	Yes

Note: All data layers may not be visible on the geologic map overview graphic.

Geologic Map Overview

The fold-out geologic map overview displays the GRI digital geologic data draped over a shaded relief image of Ebey's Landing National Historical Reserve and includes basic geographic information. For graphic clarity and legibility, not all GIS feature classes are visible on the overview. The digital elevation data and geographic information are not included with the GRI digital geologic GIS data for the park, but are available online from a variety of sources.

Map Unit Properties Table

The geologic units listed in the fold-out map unit properties table correspond to the accompanying digital geologic data. Following overall structure of the report, the table highlights the geologic issues, features, and processes associated with each map unit. The units, their relationships, and the series of events the created them are highlighted in the "Geologic History" section. Please refer to the geologic timescale (fig. 21) for the geologic period and age associated with each unit.

Use Constraints

Graphic and written information provided in this section is not a substitute for site-specific investigations, and ground-disturbing activities should neither be permitted nor denied based upon the information provided here. Minor inaccuracies may exist regarding the location of geologic features relative to other geologic or geographic features on the overview graphic. Based on the source map scale (1:24,000) and U.S. National Map Accuracy Standards, geologic features represented here are within 12 meters / 40 feet (horizontally) of their true location.

Please contact GRI with any questions.

Overview of Digital Geologic Data for Ebey's Landing NH Reserve

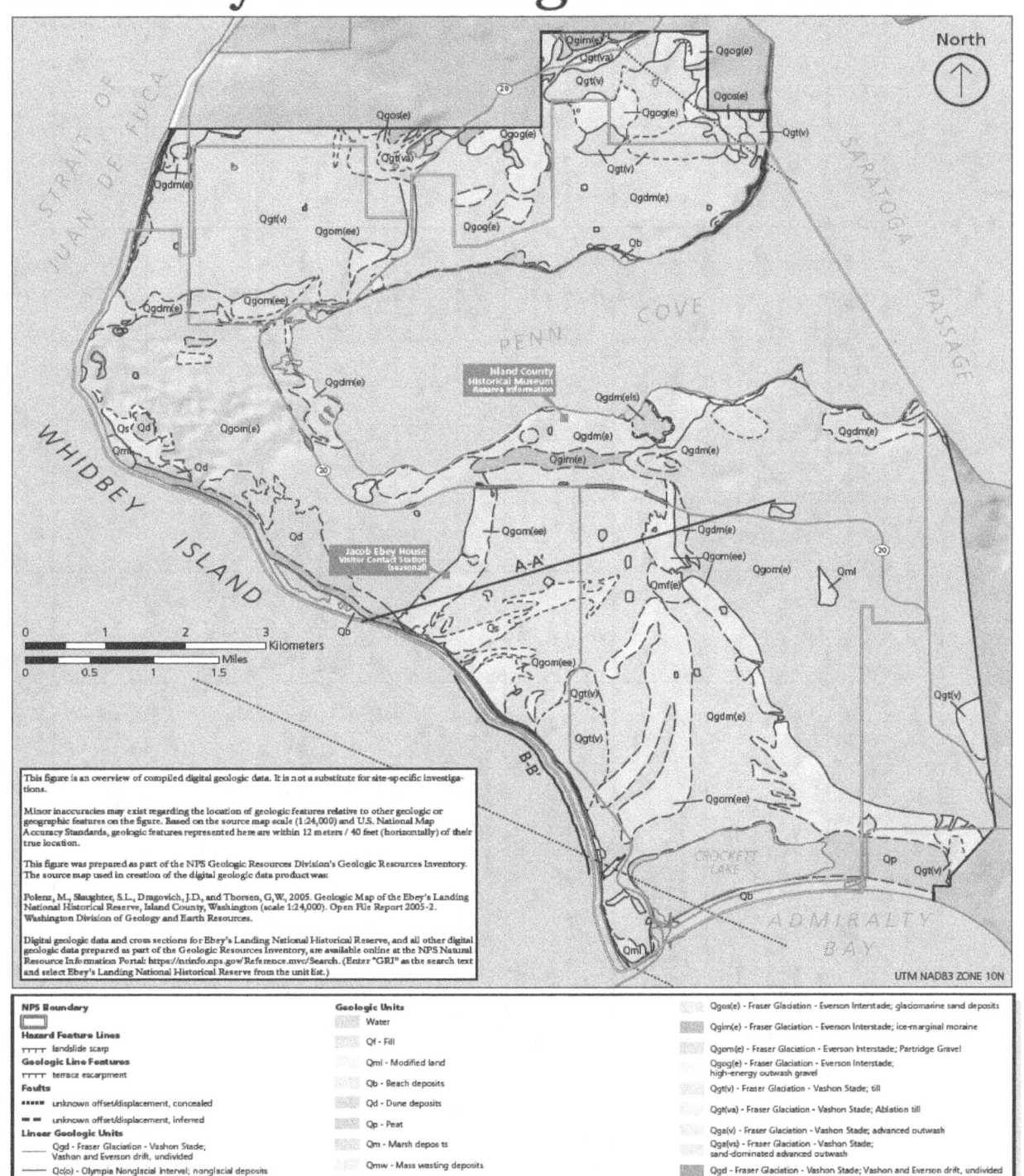

North

This figure is an overview of compiled digital geologic data. It is not a substitute for site-specific investigations.

Minor inaccuracies may exist regarding the location of geologic features relative to other geologic or geographic features on the figure. Based on the source map scale (1:24,000) and U.S. National Map Accuracy Standards, geologic features represented here are within 12 meters / 40 feet (horizontally) of their true location.

This figure was prepared as part of the NPS Geologic Resources Division's Geologic Resources Inventory. The source map used in creation of the digital geologic data product was:

Polenz, M., Slaughter, S.L., Dragovich, J.D., and Thorsen, G.W., 2005. Geologic Map of the Ebey's Landing National Historical Reserve, Island County, Washington (scale 1:24,000). Open File Report 2005-2. Washington Division of Geology and Earth Resources.

Digital geologic data and cross sections for Ebey's Landing National Historical Reserve, and all other digital geologic data prepared as part of the Geologic Resources Inventory, are available online at the NPS National Resource Information Portal: https://nrinfo.nps.gov/Reference.mvc/Search. (Enter "GRI" as the search text and select Ebey's Landing National Historical Reserve from the unit list.)

UTM NAD83 ZONE 10N

NPS Boundary

Hazard Feature Lines
- landslide scarp

Geologic Line Features
- terrace escarpment

Faults
- unknown offset/displacement, concealed
- unknown offset/displacement, inferred

Linear Geologic Units
- Qgd - Fraser Glaciation - Vashon Stade; Vashon and Everson drift, undivided
- Qc(o) - Olympia Nonglacial Interval; nonglacial deposits

Geologic Cross Section Lines
- A-A', B-B'

Geologic Contacts
- known or certain
- approximate
- inferred
- map boundary
- water or shoreline

Geologic Units
- Water
- Qf - Fill
- Qml - Modified land
- Qb - Beach deposits
- Qd - Dune deposits
- Qp - Peat
- Qm - Marsh deposits
- Qmw - Mass wasting deposits
- Qls - Landslide deposits
- Qs - Late Pleistocene sand
- Qgom(ee) - Fraser Glaciation - Everson Interstade; glaciomarine drift, emergence (beach) facies
- Qmf(e) - Fraser Glaciation - Everson Interstade; fan deposits
- Qgdm(e) - Fraser Glaciation - Everson Interstade; glaciomarine drift, undivided
- Qgdm(els) - Fraser Glaciation - Everson Interstade; landslides

- Qgos(e) - Fraser Glaciation - Everson Interstade; glaciomarine sand deposits
- Qgim(e) - Fraser Glaciation - Everson Interstade; ice-marginal moraine
- Qgom(e) - Fraser Glaciation - Everson Interstade; Partridge Gravel
- Qgog(e) - Fraser Glaciation - Everson Interstade; high-energy outwash gravel
- Qgt(v) - Fraser Glaciation - Vashon Stade; till
- Qgt(va) - Fraser Glaciation - Vashon Stade; Ablation till
- Qga(v) - Fraser Glaciation - Vashon Stade; advanced outwash
- Qga(vs) - Fraser Glaciation - Vashon Stade; sand-dominated advanced outwash
- Qgd - Fraser Glaciation - Vashon Stade; Vashon and Everson drift, undivided
- Qc(o) - Olympia Nonglacial Interval; nonglacial deposits
- Qgd(p) - Possession Glaciation; Possession Drift
- Qc(w) - Interglacial Deposits of the Whidbey Formation
- Qgd(d) - Double Bluff Glaciation; Double Bluff Drift
- Qc - Pre-Fraser Nonglacial, undivided
- Qu - Pleistocene deposits, undivided

Map Unit Properties Table: Ebey's Landing National Historical Reserve

* = Landscape Character Areas after Gilbert (1985).

Age	Map Unit (Symbol)	Geologic Description and Features	Erosion Resistance	Suitability for Infrastructure	Hazards	Paleontological Resources	Cultural Resources	Mineral Occurrence	Major Landscape Character Area*	Geological Significance
QUATERNARY (Holocene) — Historic (since about 1850)	Fill (Qf)	Clay, silt, sand, gravel, organic matter, rip-rap, and debris emplaced to elevate and reshape the land surface; includes engineered and non-engineered fills; shown where fill placement is relatively extensive, readily verifiable, and appears sufficiently thick to be of geotechnical significance. Underlies parts of Highway 28 between Kennedy's Lagoon and Penn Cove.	Variable, depending on material and subsequent vegetation.	Common by-product of development. Variable depending on material, compaction, and location.	Commonly loose, liquefiable, and prone to erosion.	None.	Represents relatively recent activities.	None.	Minor exposures in Crockett Prairie, Kettle and Pratt Woodlands, Penn Cove, San de Fuca Uplands, and West Coastal Strip.	None.
	Modified land (Qml)	Local sediment, ranging from clay to gravel, mixed and reworked by excavation and/or redistribution to modify topography; includes mappable sand and gravel pits excavated mostly into unit Qgsm(c). Mapped along western shoreline south of Partridge Point.	Variable.	Limited areal extent.	None documented; potential slumping in pits.	None.	Represents relatively recent activities.	Sand and gravel pits are remnants of mining.	Minor exposures in most areas.	None.
QUATERNARY (Pleistocene + Holocene) — Postglacial Deposits	Beach deposits (Qb)	Sand and cobbles; may include boulders, silt, pebbles, and clay; pebble-sized and larger clasts, typically well-rounded and oblate; locally well-sorted; loose; typically a mix of sediment locally derived from shoreline bluffs and underlying deposits and/or carried in by longshore drift.	Low, but replenished by longshore processes and mass wasting from upslope.	Low. Beaches tend to erode; unstable foundation.	Tides may be a potential visitor safety issue.	Unlikely, but prone to transient exposure.	Artifacts subject to intermittent exposure but unlikely to be preserved.	Quartz-rich sand.	West Coastal Strip; Crockett Prairie; Penn Cove.	Modern processes form sedimentary structures just as they did in the past.
	Dune deposits (Qd)	Hills and ridges of wind-blown sand; moderately to well sorted; deposited on upland surfaces and in kettle sidewalls along or near west-facing shoreline bluffs north of Ebey's Landing. Age estimates indicate deposition of some dunes began during the early Holocene. Dune morphology suggests that the depositional environment lacked the forests that cover most of these dunes today, but minimal soil development and location of the dunes within 0.8 km (0.5 mi) of the present-day shoreline bluffs suggest deposition may also be recent and ongoing. Estimated radiocarbon ages of 8,840 ±50 and 8,280 ±40 years before present (BP). Located near unstable shoreline bluffs; north of Ebey's Landing.	Low.	Low.	No significant hazards.	Kettle filled with wind-blown sands contained snails, birds, and a variety of mammalian bones.	Artifacts unlikely to be preserved due to exposure.	Quartz-rich sand.	Kettle and Pratt Woodlands.	Fossils may represent only known record of continental animals from Pacific Northwest during early Holocene (Mustoe et al. 2005).
	Peat (Qp)	Organic and organic-matter-rich mineral sediments deposited in closed depressions; includes peat, muck, silt, and clay in and adjacent to wetlands; unit Qp is the freshwater equivalent of unit Qm and may locally grade down to that unit. Isolated deposits in kettles and near Crockett Lake lowlands. Typically, associated with wetlands in modern environment.	High. Low energy setting saturated and stabilized by organic matter.	Low.	Prone to intense shaking during earthquakes.	Possible Holocene plant, vertebrate and invertebrate remains.	Artifacts may be buried in peat.	Peat.	Crockett Prairie.	May convert to lignite or coal with increased pressure, temperature, and time.
	Marsh deposits (Qm)	Organic and organic-matter-rich mineral sediments deposited in a saltwater or brackish-marsh (estuarine or lagoonal) environment. Mapped near shorelines. Isolated with limited areal extent.	High. Water saturated, low-energy environment.	Low.	Prone to intense shaking and liquefaction during earthquakes.	Possible Holocene plant, vertebrate and invertebrate remains.	Artifacts may be buried in marsh.	None.	Minor units in West Coastal Strip, San de Fuca Uplands.	Post-glacial record of land level and/or sea level history.
	Mass wasting deposits (Qmw)	Boulders, gravel, sand, silt, and clay; generally unsorted but may be locally stratified; typically loose; shown along mostly colluvium-covered or densely vegetated slopes that are demonstrably unstable or appear potentially unstable; contains exposures of underlying units and landslides that cannot be mapped with confidence or are too small to show as separate features. Unstable, ephemeral deposits along bluffs.	Low.	Low. Unstable deposits.	Potential reactivation of unstable slopes.	Unlikely. Transient deposits.	Low potential for preservation of artifacts.	None.	Minor unit mapped in coastal areas.	Reflects processes that occurred along shorelines in the past.

Age	Map Unit (Symbol)	Geologic Description and Features	Erosion Resistance	Suitability for Infrastructure	Hazards	Paleontological Resources	Cultural Resources	Mineral Occurrence	Major Landscape Character Area*	Geological Significance
QUATERNARY (Pleistocene+Holocene) — Postglacial Deposits	Landslide deposit (Qls)	Gravel, sand, silt, clay, and boulders in slide body and toe, and underlying units in scarp areas, angular to rounded clasts unsorted; generally loose, unstratified, broken, and chaotic, but may locally retain primary bedding; may include liquefaction features; deposited by mass-wasting processes other than soil creep and frost heave; typically unconformable with surrounding units; includes active and inactive slides shown where scale permits. Absence of a mapped slide does not imply absence of sliding or hazard. Unstable ephemeral deposits along bluffs.	Low. Wave action along beaches removes most slide deposits.	Low. Unstable deposits.	All shoreline bluffs are subject to episodic landsliding and resultant bluff retreat.	Unlikely. Transient deposits.	Low potential for preservation of artifacts.	None.	Minor unit mapped in coastal areas.	Reflects processes that occurred along shorelines in the past.
	Late Pleistocene sand (Qs)	Fine sand to silt; light gray where fresh, light-tan to reddish brown where weathered; moderately well sorted; blankets much of the map area as 0.2–1.2 m (0.5–4 ft) thick sheet that typically forms topsoil; mapped only where thickness appears to exceed 1.5 m (5 ft); well to very well drained; grain size, sorting, and morphology suggest wind-blown origin for some exposures, but elsewhere, mineralogy, poor sorting, and high angularity suggest till or glaciomarine drift [Qgdm(e), Qgt(v), and Qgt(va)] or mixed sources; appears to represent a postglacial, late Pleistocene pulse of sedimentation because it is stratigraphically beneath, and typically separated by a paleosol from Holocene dunes (Qd) that lack a similar degree of soil development.	Low except where stabilized by vegetation on relatively flat topography inland from Ebey's Landing.	Suitable for roads and infrastructure, but limited mappable exposures.	None.	Unlikely.	Unknown. Probable archaeological sites.	Quartz-rich sand.	Ebey's Prairie.	Paleosol in top of unit may reflect a late Pleistocene to early Holocene climate conducive to more rapid soil development than today's modern climate.
QUATERNARY (Pleistocene) — Deposits of the Fraser Glaciation (Everson Interstade)	Glacio-marine drift, beach facies [Qgom(ee)]	Sand and gravel, locally silty; loose; typically only a few feet thick; underlain by Qgdm(e) or Qgom(e), but may rest on older sediments north and west of Penn Cove and along parts of the slope east of Ebey's Prairie. Characteristic subtle benches at varying elevations represent paleo-beach berms. Contains the youngest facies of glaciomarine drift but may also include terrestrial deposits. Mapped as outwash to maintain continuity with maps to the north. Underlies roads and buildings at Fort Casey.	Variable. Typically well-drained and stabilized by vegetation.	Suitable for roads and infrastructure.	None.	Unlikely.	Unknown. Potential for archaeological sites.	Sand and gravel.	Crockett Prairie, Ebey's Prairie, Fort Casey Uplands, San de Fuca Uplands.	Emergent deposits record a falling relative sea level at the end of the Everson Interstade.
	Fan deposits [Qmf(e)]	Sand, fine gravel, silt, and clay; variably sorted; loose; bedded; consists of either terrigenous nearshore marine deltaic or terrestrial alluvial fans that record a late Everson Interstade (?), onshore hydrologic regime conducive to surface runoff in loose, well-drained units like Qgom(e); located at the foot of small, relict valleys that lack modern streams and were incised into Qgom(e) or other easily eroded deposits. If unit deposition is tied to sea level change, valley incision and fan deposition ceased when relative sea level dropped sufficiently below the head of the fan to cause the groundwater table to lower, resulting in termination of surface runoff capable of incision. Valley incision into and fan deposition on the delta front landform in Qgom(e) indicate that Partridge Gravel deposition had locally ceased; thus, the ice front that had supplied the water that deposited the Partridge Gravel had locally reduced meltwater supply, and the runoff that deposited unit Qmf(e) near Coupeville was likely fed by other sources. Best viewed as neither glaciomarine drift nor outwash, although deposition was likely coeval (and may interfinger) with nearby deposition of glaciomarine drift. Assigned to the Everson Interstade based on presumed association with Everson sea level. Mapped in three fan-shaped exposures of limited areal extent.	Variable. More resistant to erosion where the unit has been stabilized by vegetation.	Low due to minor exposures of limited areal extent. The largest area contains a road and buildings.	None.	Unlikely.	Unknown. Limited areal extent.	Quartz-rich sand and gravel.	Minor unit with limited areal extent mapped along the southwestern border of Parker and Patmore Woodlands.	May mark a climatic shift or an elevated (but dropping) relative sea level late in the Everson Interstade.

* = Landscape Character Areas after Gilbert (1985).

Age	Map Unit (Symbol)	Geologic Description and Features	Erosion Resistance	Suitability for Infrastructure	Hazards	Paleontological Resources	Cultural Resources	Mineral Occurrence	Major Landscape Character Area*	Geological Significance
QUATERNARY (Pleistocene) — Deposits of the Fraser Glaciation (Everson Interstade)	Glaciomarine drift, undivided [Qgdm(e)] Landslides [Qgdm(els)]	Qgdm(e): Clayey to silty diamicton with variable content of gravel-sized clasts; also includes silt, clay, sand, and combinations thereof; contains marine shells; weathered color most commonly buff but ranges to olive-gray, ash-gray, or white; dark-gray where unweathered; dry face characteristically includes vertical desiccation cracks with dark-brown staining; massive to rhythmically bedded, commonly with sharp upper and lower, unit-bounding unconformities; mostly loose and soft but locally hard and compact. Some exposures are very like till, but till generally lacks fossils, and glaciomarine drift generally has a finer-grained, smoother-feeling matrix, and is more likely to be stratified, more likely to be buff-colored, and typically less compact (and less water-restrictive) than till. Till-like deposits are most prominent along elevated portions of Blowers Bluff, the north shore of Penn Cove, and the cliff between Ebey's Landing and Fort Casey. Locally divided into Qgdm(els). Qgdm(els): Apparent landslides that lack evidence of recent activity. Dominated by glaciomarine drift material that may be slightly looser than glaciomarine drift outside the slump area. May be Everson Interstade(?) submarine(?) slumps that do not necessarily pose a slide hazard.	High where stabilized by vegetation as in Ebey's Prairie; variable along bluffs.	High. Underlies unimproved and improved roads, buildings, and towns.	Commonly forms vertical faces prone to sudden failure along desiccation cracks.	Contains marine shells; one shell yielded a radiocarbon date of 13,650 years BP.	Unknown. Potential for archaeological sites.	None (diamicton).	Major map unit. Includes: Coupeville, Crockett Prairie, Ebey's Prairie, Fort Casey Uplands, San de Fuca Uplands.	Consists of sea-floor sediment, and its variegated character appears to reflect initial proximity of the ice front. Age spans the entire Everson Interstade.
	Glaciomarine sand deposits [Qgos(e)]	Sand, pebbly sand, and silty fine sand with locally thin interbeds of silt and rare cobbly sand; mostly structureless to locally plane-bedded, laminated, or rarely cross-bedded; locally completely interlayered with other glaciomarine drift; includes minor glaciofluvial deposits. Fining trends and sedimentary structures suggest deposition in a shallow glaciomarine setting such as foreshore deposits or submarine fan turbidites. Except for minor areas along the northern border of the reserve, the unit is mapped north of the reserve.	Low, except where stabilized by vegetation.	Underlies roads and buildings. Potential farmland.	None.	Unlikely, but may contain marine shells.	Potential for archaeological sites.	Sand.	Part of the San de Fuca Uplands, but mostly mapped north of the reserve, which does not have defined landscape areas.	Sedimentary structures suggest a shallow glacio-marine or sub-marine fan turbidite depositional environment.
	Ice-marginal moraine [Qgim(e)]	Cobbly to bouldery, angular to rounded gravel with loose, powdery matrix, abundant void spaces, and abundant erratics on the surface; forms a gentle, 150–240 m (500–800 ft)–wide east-west ridge across Coupeville; marks the ice margin during Everson Interstade, likely deposited before the shell dated in Qgdm(e).	High. Stabilized by vegetation.	High. Underlies roads, buildings, and infrastructure.	None.	Highly unlikely.	Unknown. Potential for archaeological sites.	Gravel.	Coupeville.	Ice margin during the early part of the Everson Interstade.
	Partridge Gravel [Qgom(e)]	Sand, gravel, and sand-gravel mixtures with minor interlayered silt and silty sand; at least 64 m (210 ft) thick above sea level southeast of Partridge Point, with well records locally suggesting an additional 41 m (135 ft) below sea level; forms angle-of-repose slopes, such as at Partridge Point. Includes three outwash facies that compose an upward-coarsening, marine, kame-delta-turbidite complex: 1) a mostly horizontally bedded, sand-dominated, bottom-set sea floor facies with common low-energy gravity flow cross-bedding, flame structures, and other soft sediment deformation features, but apparently lacking dropstones; 2) an overlying foreset-bedded sand and gravel facies; and 3) a capping, top-set, channelized gravel and sand facies that coarsens locally to a bouldery gravel and reflects a shallow-water deltaic to subaerial, braided-stream environment with abundant cut-and-fill cross-bedding. Many exposures of the bottom-set sand facies include sparse, randomly distributed inclusions and apparently gravity-sorted trains of sand- to fine-gravel-sized, detrital fragments of peat, charred wood, charcoal, coal, pumice, and dacite. Tephra deposits may be re-worked from nearby units, mostly Qc(o). Assuming an average thickness of 30–76 m (100–250 ft), the unit holds about 0.8 to 2.5 km³ (0.2 to 0.6 mi³) of sand and gravel. Areally extensive throughout the reserve especially in the Partridge Point area, north of Ebey's Landing, and Smith Prairie.	Variable. Low along some bluffs. Moderate where the unit forms relatively stable angle-of-repose slopes, and high where stabilized by vegetation on relatively flat topography.	High. Underlies structures.	Unstable along some slopes, especially where undercut.	Possible invertebrate shells preserved in marine facies.	Potential for archaeological sites.	Sand and gravel. Outwash sand and gravel are important sources for concrete and construction uses south of Seattle.	Primary map unit in Parker and Patmore Wood-lands and Smith Prairie. One of two major map units in Kettle and Pratt Woodlands and West Coastal Strip.	Type section is at Partridge Point. Tephra chemistry and field relations favor a Glacier Peak origin for tephra (may be reworked from older geologic deposits). Age is early Everson Interstade, sometime after the initial incursion of marine water into the Puget Lowland but predating the marine shell in Qgdm(e) dating to 13,650 ±390 years BP.

* = Landscape Character Areas after Gilbert (1985).

Age	Map Unit (Symbol)	Geologic Description and Features	Erosion Resistance	Suitability for Infrastructure	Hazards	Paleontological Resources	Cultural Resources	Mineral Occurrence	Major Landscape Character Area*	Geological Significance
Deposits of the Fraser Glaciation (Everson Interstade)	High-energy outwash gravel [Qgog(e)]	Diverse deposit of gravel with lenses of sand, silt, and clay and inclusions of boulder-sized, subangular to well-rounded silt and clay derived from massive to well-bedded, compact, pre-Fraser deposits of fine sediment; crudely to well bedded, locally unbedded, and commonly including steep bedding, gravelly incisions (intrusions?) into underlying units, and other indicators of a high-energy flow regime; typically supports vertical bluff faces but locally forms angle-of-repose slopes; widely exposed beneath Qgdm(e) along the Penn Cove shoreline between Coupeville and Blowers Bluff, where it steeply truncates at least 12 m (40 ft) of pre-Fraser section. Like Qgom(e), unit is overlain by Qgdm(e). Southwest of Penn Cove, locally grades up into and thus is a lateral facies equivalent of the Partridge Gravel. For that reason and because the unit is apparently nowhere overlain by convincing exposures of Vashon Till (Qgt(v)), assigned to the Everson Interstade. Separated from Partridge Gravel because Partridge Gravel is marine-deltaic and lacks the characteristics of high-energy flow that mark this unit. The unit is not areally extensive and is primarily present within vertical bluffs along the shoreline of Penn Cove.	Low to moderate. Erodes to angle-of-repose slopes. Primarily shoreline deposits that may be exposed to wave erosion.	Low. Limited areal extent.	The unit is part of vertical bluff faces that may collapse.	None.	Unlikely due to limited exposures within the vertical bluffs.	Gravel, but not extensive in the reserve. South of Seattle, outwash sand and gravel are important sources of raw materials for concrete and construction.	Minor unit with limited areal extent. Mapped in Kettle and Pratt Woodlands, Penn Cove, and San de Fuca Uplands.	Interpreted as dominantly a subglacial flow deposit, except in upland areas between Route 20 and Penn Cove near the northern boundary of the map, where the depositional and temporal-stratigraphic setting is unclear.
QUATERNARY (Pleistocene) — Deposits of the Fraser Glaciation (Vashon Stade)	Till [Qgt(v)]; Ablation till [Qgt(va)]; Advanced outwash [Qga(v), Qga(vs)]	Primarily mapped north of Penn Cove. Qgt(v): Mix of clay, silt, sand, and gravel; gray where fresh, light yellowish-brown where oxidized; unsorted; highly compacted, but locally clast supported; very low permeability; commonly matrix-supported, but locally clast supported; matrix more angular than water-worked sediments, resulting in a grittier feel than the matrix of Qgdm(e); cobbles and boulders commonly faceted and/or striated; forms a patchy cover varying from less than 0.15 m (0.5 ft) to greater than 15 m (50 ft) thick, with thicknesses of 3–9 m (10–30 ft) most common; may include outwash and ablation till that are too thin to map separately. Lies between overlying Qgdm(e) and underlying Qga(v) and Qga(vs). Stratigraphic position relative to Qgog(e) remains unresolved. May include local exposures of older till similar in stratigraphic position, lithology, and appearance.

Qgt(va): Unsorted, unstratified melt-out deposit of loose gravel, sand, silt, and clay. | High, resembling concrete where well-developed, but exposures along bluffs can be unstable. | High. Underlies roads, buildings, and other infrastructure. | Forms vertical faces in coastal bluffs along Penn Cove shoreline and thus may contribute to bluff collapse. | None. | Unlikely. Unit was deposited by a glacier when the region was covered beneath thousands of feet of ice. | Potential landscaping material (boulders). | Fort Casey Uplands; San de Fuca Uplands. | Deposited as diamicton directly by Vashon Stade glacier ice.

Local and nearby age control constrains the age of the unit to between about 18,000 years BP and sometime before deposition of the shell in Qgdm(e) that dates to 13,650 ±350 years BP. |
| Deposits of the Fraser Glaciation (Vashon Stade) | Advanced outwash [Qga(v), Qga(vs)] | Qga(v): Sand and pebble to cobble gravel with some bouldery facies; local silt and clay; may contain till fragments; gray to grayish-brown and grayish-orange; clasts well-rounded; typically well-sorted and clean except in some ice-proximal deposits near the top of the unit; compact, but in many exposures only minimally cohesive; parallel-bedded, locally cross-bedded; less than 6 m (20 ft) thick in most exposures; commonly overlain by Qgt(v), along a sharp contact and stratigraphically above Qc(o); commonly forms angle-of-repose benches within coastal bluffs. Locally divided into Qga(vs).

Qga(vs): Sand-dominated advance outwash. May overlie impermeable deposits on steep slopes. | Variable. Exposures are too limited in areal extent to map. Finer sediment tends to erode more readily than coarser-grained material. | Low due to few exposures and limited areal extent. | Forms angle-of-repose benches within coastal bluffs. May contribute to landslides and bluff retreat. Qga(vs) is prone to sudden landslides along steep slopes. | Not recognized to be fossiliferous in the reserve, but contains mammoth remains in British Columbia | Unknown and unlikely. Depositional environment very inhospitable and dynamic. | Sand and gravel. | Minor unit mapped along the coastline of Penn Cove and West Coastal Strip. | Age is bracketed to between about 20,000 and 18,000 years BP by local and nearby age control from within the underlying Qc(o) and an estimate of Vashon ice arrival |

Age	Map Unit (Symbol)	Geologic Description and Features	Erosion Resistance	Suitability for Infrastructure	Hazards	Paleontological Resources	Cultural Resources	Mineral Occurrence	Major Landscape Character Area*	Geological Significance
QUATERNARY (Pleistocene)	**Everson Interstade and Vashon Stade** Vashon and Everson drift, undivided (Qgd)	Glaciomarine drift [Qgdm(e)], till [Qgt(v)], and advance outwash [Qga(v)] and Qga(vs)] combined into single unit where map scale or exposure do not permit separate presentation. Only two exposures are mapped along the western bluff.	See specific units	Low. Limited areal extent.	Bluff collapse.	None.	Unknown. Limited areal extent.	Patchy sand, gravel, and boulders.	Minor unit mapped along West Coastal Strip.	See specific units
	Deposits of the Olympia Nonglacial Interval: Olympia Nonglacial Interval [Qc(o)]	Silt, clay, sand, and local lenses and interbeds of fine gravel; includes the West Beach (north of Partridge Point) silt facies interpreted as loess; typically horizontally bedded to massive; commonly forms vertical bluffs; silt facies locally contain sparse gastropod fossils. Petrographic study indicates that alluvial facies reflect ancestral Skagit River provenance. Sparse, local Glacier Peak dacite and pumice pebbles, such as those found to the east of Long Point are chemically indistinguishable from lahar runout deposits within the Whidbey Formation [Qc(w)], but no lahar runout deposits were recognized in Qc(o). Age of the West Beach silt is constrained in the map area to about 37,000 to 27,000 years BP by radiocarbon dates from overlying and underlying units. May include fine-grained early Vashon advance deposits, such as at north Penn Cove, where the upper radiocarbon date and sedimentary characteristics of overlying silty sediment may be compatible with the early Vashon Stade. The limited exposures of overlying silty sediment are mapped within bluffs along the western shore and at Blowers Bluff.	Low. Subject to wave and storm activity.	Low due to limited accessibility.	Exposed in vertical bluffs and thus may contribute to bluff collapse along coastline.	Gastropod fossils. Mastodon tusk (proboscidean) found south of Ebey's Prairie. Plant fossils and pollen.	Unlikely (pre-Fraser and glacial).	None.	Minor unit that is mapped along the coastline of Penn Cove and the West Coastal Strip.	The age of the entire unit may be limited to between about 37,000 and 16,800 years BP by six radiocarbon dates and the age of the West Beach silt. However, undated strata within the unit may include significantly older deposits.
	Deposits of the Possession Glaciation: Possession Drift [Qgd(p)]	Glaciomarine drift facies: Highly diverse; typically clayey silt, silty clay, clay, and clay-rich diamicton; buff, ranging to ash gray or white; compact and commonly with vertical desiccation cracks; contains shells; more compact than Everson Interstade equivalent; locally indistinguishable from till. Till facies: Typically sandy diamicton; ash gray to white; compact. Outwash sand facies: Gray, medium to fine grained sand. Classified as advance. Mostly glaciomarine drift along Blowers Bluff; dominantly sand at West Beach and within 2.4 km (1.5 mi) southeast of Ebey's Landing, but glaciomarine drift overlies till farther south along the same bluff. Sand at West Beach is very similar to and was distinguished from underlying channel sand of Qc(w) based on petrographic determination of mineralogical content. The unit is within vertical bluffs along the western shore (West Beach) and at Blowers Bluff.	Variable. The glaciomarine facies is more resistant than the outwash sand facies.	Low. The unit lies within vertical bluffs	Erosion of the unit may under-cut the bluff and influence bluff collapse and retreat.	Shells.	Unlikely (pre-Fraser and glacial).	None.	Minor unit mapped along the coastline of Penn Cove and the West Coastal Strip.	Type section: Possession Point, South Whidbey Island. Distinguished from equivalent Fraser Glaciation units by stratigraphic position. Estimated age of about 80,000-60,000 years BP.
	Interglacial Deposits of the Whidbey Formation: Whidbey Formation [Qc(w)]	Sand, silt, clay, peat layers, occasional fine gravel, and rare medium gravel; exposures commonly weathered to a subtly multicolored to light-yellow hue. Basal flood-plain facies overlain by a channel sand facies. Flood-plain facies: Typically 3–6 m (10–20 ft) thick, well stratified (subhorizontally), and commonly slightly oxidized. Contains discontinuous peat beds. At least 9 m (30 ft) thick along West Beach, but descends 900 m (3,000 ft) below sea level to the southern flood-plain facies. Channel sand facies: Roughly 9 m (30 ft) thick, clean, gray, cross-bedded to massive. Resembles the overlying Qgd(p) so that petrographic analysis may be necessary to distinguish these two units. At Blowers Bluff, the flood-plain facies reaches a maximum thickness of 8 m (25 ft) and is overlain by a gravelly, cross-bedded channel sand facies that is lavender to light yellowish-gray, 4.5–24 m (15–80 ft) thick, and prone to forming angle-of-repose benches at Blowers Bluff and an angle-of-repose cliff at West Beach. Local concentrations of dacite and pumice pebble trains come from Glacier Peak lahar runout deposits. Age is about 125,000-80,000 years BP.	Low. Forms the base of the section along the shoreline bluffs of West Beach and Blowers Bluff and thus is subject to wave and storm energy.	Low. The flood-plain facies forms prominent vertical bluffs, which are too unstable for development.	Erosion of the unit may under-cut the bluff and influence bluff collapse and retreat.	May contain pachyderm fossils, such as the mammoth tusk discovered in Qc(o).	Unlikely (pre-Fraser and glacial).	Sand and peat.	Minor unit mapped along the coastline of Penn Cove and San de Fuca Uplands.	Type section: Double Bluff, south Whidbey Island. Informally named the lahar runout of Oak Harbor in Oak Harbor 7.5-minute quadrangle north of the reserve. Mineralogical composition indicates an ancestral Skagit River basin provenance.

Age	Map Unit (Symbol)	Geologic Description and Features	Erosion Resistance	Suitability for Infrastructure	Hazards	Paleontological Resources	Cultural Resources	Mineral Occurrence	Major Landscape Character Area*	Geological Significance
QUATERNARY (Pleistocene)	Deposits of the Double Bluff Glaciation: Double Bluff Drift [Qgd(d)]	Glaciomarine drift (silt, clay, and diamicton) and locally underlying till; resembles equivalent Vashon Drift units but is assigned to the Double Bluff Glaciation based on stratigraphic position; lithology reflects British Columbian provenance. Only mapped along 460 m (1,500 ft) of shoreline southeast of Ebey's Landing. Limited to exposures along the shoreline southeast of Ebey's Landing.	Low. Till facies commonly resembles concrete, but unit is subject to wave and storm activity.	Low. Limited exposures	Erosion of the unit may influence bluff collapse.	Unknown.	Unlikely (pre-Fraser and glacial).	None.	Minor unit mapped along the West Coastal Strip.	Type section: Double Bluff, south Whidbey Island. About 185,000–125,000 years BP.
	Pre-Fraser Nonglacial, undivided (Qc)	Sand, silt, clay, peat, some fine gravel, and rare medium gravel, well stratified to massive. Resembles Qc(o) and Qc(w). Thought to be nonglacial but may locally include glacial material. Lies below Fraser glacial deposits of unknown age and association. One exposure is mapped along the north shore of Penn Cove, about 900 m (3,000 ft) west of columnar section 4.	Variable lithology. Subject to wave action.	Not applicable. Only one exposure.	Isolated exposure, but erosion of unit may influence bluff collapse.	May contain pachyderm fossils, such as the mammoth tusk discovered in Qc(o).	Unlikely (pre-Fraser and glacial).	Sand and peat.	Minor unit mapped along Penn Cove coastline.	Olympia or Whidbey age, but older origin is possible.
	Pleistocene deposits, undivided (Qu)	Limited to three isolate exposures on the map. Unknown age and association. Exposure west of Long Point (columnar section 6) consists of a 22-m (73-ft)- thick section of gray, medium- to fine-grained, subangular to sub rounded, poorly sorted, compact to mildly compact, plane- to gently cross-bedded, lithologically diverse sand with sparsely disseminated, thin (< 1 in. (2.54 cm) thick] elongate pockets of granule-sized pumice and coal; soft-sediment deformation structures and/or liquefaction features are exposed in the basal 6 m (20 ft) of section 6; sand is interlayered with at least three compact, discontinuous, greenish-olive to dark gray diamictons up to 2 m (6 ft) thick, with sparse to rare, subrounded to angular granule to pebble clasts. Grains angular to subangular. Mixed lithology does not indicate a specific source area or glacial or interglacial conditions. Angularity of particles in diamicton suggests till. A separate exposure 0.5 km (0.3 mi) southwest of the Coupeville dock consists of compact, quartz-rich sand. Includes an exposure of somewhat compact cobble gravel near the top of a hill 1,200 m (4,000 ft) southeast of Lovejoy Point. Exposure is in the sideslope of a hill that rises about 3 m (10 ft) above the surrounding glaciomarine drift and recessional outwash gravel, suggesting that the hill is cored with older sediment.	Lower resistance to erosion along Penn Cove coastline where the unit is subject to wave activity	Not applicable. Isolated exposures.	Isolated exposure, but erosion of unit along shore may influence bluff collapse.	May contain pachyderm fossils, such as the mammoth tusk discovered in Qc(o).	Unlikely (pre-Fraser and glacial).	Sand. Minute inclusions of detrital coal.	Minor unit mapped in Coupeville, Parker and Pratt Wood-lands, and Penn Cove.	May include both glacial and interglacial deposits.

Glossary

This glossary contains brief definitions of technical geologic terms used in this report. Not all geologic terms used are referenced. For more detailed definitions or to find terms not listed here please visit: http://geomaps.wr.usgs.gov/parks/misc/glossarya.html. Definitions are based on those in the American Geological Institute Glossary of Geology (fifth edition; 2005).

ablation. All processes by which snow and ice are lost from a glacier, including melting, evaporation (sublimation), wind erosion, and calving.

ablation till. Loosely consolidated rock debris, formerly in or on a glacier, that accumulated in place as the surface ice was removed by ablation.

absolute age. The geologic age of a fossil, rock, feature, or event in years; commonly refers to radiometrically determined ages.

active margin. A tectonically active margin where lithospheric plates come together (convergent boundary), pull apart (divergent boundary) or slide past one another (transform boundary). Typically associated with earthquakes and, in the case of convergent and divergent boundaries, volcanism. Compare to "passive margin."

alpine glacier. A glacier occurring in a mountainous region; also called a valley glacier.

aquifer. A rock or sedimentary unit that is sufficiently porous that it has a capacity to hold water, sufficiently permeable to allow water to move through it, and currently saturated to some level.

asthenosphere. Earth's relatively weak layer or shell below the rigid lithosphere.

beach. A gently sloping shoreline covered with sediment, commonly formed by the action of waves and tides.

beach face. The section of the beach exposed to direct wave and/or tidal action.

bed. The smallest sedimentary strata unit, commonly ranging in thickness from one centimeter to a meter or two and distinguishable from beds above and below.

bedding. Depositional layering or stratification of sediments.

bedrock. A general term for the rock that underlies soil or other unconsolidated, surficial material.

block (fault). A crustal unit bounded by faults, either completely or in part.

braided stream. A sediment-clogged stream that forms multiple channels which divide and rejoin.

calcareous. Describes rock or sediment that contains the mineral calcium carbonate ($CaCO_3$).

cementation. Chemical precipitation of material into pores between grains that bind the grains into rock.

chemical sediment. A sediment precipitated directly from solution (also called nonclastic).

clast. An individual grain or rock fragment in a sedimentary rock, produced by the physical disintegration of a larger rock mass.

clastic. Describes rock or sediment made of fragments of pre-existing rocks (clasts).

clay. Can be used to refer to clay minerals or as a sedimentary fragment size classification (less than 1/256 mm [0.00015 in]).

claystone. Lithified clay having the texture and composition of shale but lacking shale's fine layering and fissility (characteristic splitting into thin layers).

cordillera. A Spanish term for an extensive mountain range; used in North America to refer to all of the western mountain ranges of the continent.

craton. The relatively old and geologically stable interior of a continent (also see "continental shield").

cross-bedding. Uniform to highly varied sets of inclined sedimentary beds deposited by wind or water that indicate flow conditions such as water flow direction and depth.

crust. Earth's outermost compositional shell, 10 to 40 km (6 to 25 mi) thick, consisting predominantly of relatively low-density silicate minerals (also see "oceanic crust" and "continental crust").

deformation. A general term for the process of faulting, folding, and shearing of rocks as a result of various Earth forces such as compression (pushing together) and extension (pulling apart).

delta. A sediment wedge deposited where a stream flows into a lake or sea.

diamictite (diamicton). Poorly sorted, noncalcareous, sedimentary rock with a wide range of particle sizes.

dip. The angle between a bed or other geologic surface and horizontal.

drift. All rock material (clay, silt, sand, gravel, boulders) transported by a glacier and deposited directly by or from the ice, or by running water emanating from a glacier. Includes unstratified material (till) and stratified deposits (outwash plains and fluvial deposits). Also includes glaciomarine lake and seafloor sediments marked by contributions from nearby glacial settings (e.g., ice bergs).

dropstone. An oversized stone in laminated sediment that depresses the underlying laminae and may be covered by other laminae that drape over the stone. Most originate through ice-rafting; other sources include floating tree roots.

drumlin. A low, smoothly rounded, elongate oval hill, mound, or ridge of compact glacial till built under the margin of the ice and shaped by its flow with its long axis parallel to the direction of ice movement.

dune. A low mound or ridge of sediment, usually sand, deposited by wind.

eolian. Formed, eroded, or deposited by or related to the action of the wind. Also spelled "aeolian."

extrusive. Describes igneous material that has erupted onto Earth's surface.

facies (sedimentary). The depositional or environmental conditions reflected in the sedimentary structures, textures, mineralogy, fossils, etc. of a sedimentary rock.

fault. A break in rock along which relative movement has occurred between the two sides.

flame structure. A sedimentary structure consisting of wave- or flame-shaped plumes of mud that have been squeezed irregularly upward into an overlying layer.

footwall. The mass of rock beneath a fault surface (also see "hanging wall").

formation. Fundamental rock-stratigraphic unit that is mappable, lithologically distinct from adjoining strata, and has definable upper and lower contacts.

glacial erratic. Boulders transported by glaciers some distance from their point of origin.

glaciomarine. The accumulation of glacially eroded, terrestrially derived sediment in the marine environment.

hanging wall. The mass of rock above a fault surface (also see "footwall").

ice-rafting. The transporting of rock fragments of all sizes on or within icebergs, ice floes, or other forms of floating ice.

igneous. Refers to a rock or mineral that originated from molten material; one of the three main classes of rocks—igneous, metamorphic, and sedimentary.

intrusion. A body of igneous rock that invades (pushes into) older rock. The invading rock may be a plastic solid or magma.

jameo. A large collapse sink formed by collapse of the roof of more than one level of a multi-level lava tube cave.

kame delta. A flat-topped, steep-sided hill of well-sorted sand and gravel deposited by a meltwater stream flowing into a proglacial or other ice-marginal lake. The proximal margin of the delta was built in contact with glacier ice.

lacustrine. Pertaining to, produced by, or inhabiting a lake or lakes.

lahar. A mudflow (mass movement) composed primarily of volcaniclastic materials on the flank of a volcano. The debris carried in the flow includes pyroclasts, blocks from primary lava flows, and clastic material.

landslide. Any process or landform resulting from rapid, gravity-driven mass movement.

lithification. The conversion of sediment into solid rock.

lithify. To change to stone or to petrify; especially to consolidate from a loose sediment to a solid rock through compaction and cementation.

lithosphere. The relatively rigid outmost shell of Earth's structure, 50 to 100 km (31 to 62 miles) thick, that encompasses the crust and uppermost mantle.

lodgment till. The plastering beneath a glacier of successive layers of basal till commonly characterized by compact fissile structure and containing stones oriented with their long axes generally parallel to the direction of ice movement.

loess. Windblown silt-sized sediment, generally of glacial origin.

longshore current. A current parallel to a coastline caused by waves approaching the shore at an oblique angle.

matrix. The fine grained material between coarse (larger) grains in igneous rocks or poorly sorted clastic sediments or rocks. Also refers to rock or sediment in which a fossil is embedded.

meander. Sinuous lateral curve or bend in a stream channel. An entrenched meander is incised, or carved downward into the surface of the valley in which a meander originally formed. The meander preserves its original pattern with little modification.

mechanical weathering. The physical breakup of rocks without change in composition. Synonymous with "physical weathering."

member. A lithostratigraphic unit with definable contacts; a member subdivides a formation.

meta–. A prefix used with the name of a sedimentary or igneous rock, indicating that the rock has been metamorphosed.

metamorphic. Describes the process of metamorphism or its results. One of the three main classes of rocks—igneous, metamorphic, and sedimentary.

mineral. A naturally occurring, inorganic crystalline solid with a definite chemical composition or compositional range.

mud cracks. Cracks formed in clay, silt, or mud by shrinkage during dehydration at Earth's surface.

normal fault. A dip-slip fault in which the hanging wall moves down relative to the footwall.

oceanic crust. Earth's crust formed at spreading ridges that underlies the ocean basins. Oceanic crust is 6 to 7 km (3 to 4 miles) thick and generally of basaltic composition.

orogeny. A mountain-building event.

outcrop. Any part of a rock mass or formation that is exposed or "crops out" at Earth's surface.

outwash. Glacial sediment transported and deposited by meltwater streams.

paleogeography. The study, description, and reconstruction of the physical landscape from past geologic periods.

paleosol. A ancient soil layer preserved in the geologic record.

passive margin. A margin where no plate-scale tectonism is taking place; plates are not converging, diverging, or sliding past one another. An example is the east coast of North America. (also see "active margin").

pebble. Generally, small rounded rock particles from 4 to 64 mm (0.16 to 2.52 in) in diameter.

permeability. A measure of the relative ease with which fluids move through the pore spaces of rocks or sediments.

plate tectonics. The concept that the lithosphere is broken up into a series of rigid plates that move over Earth's surface above a more fluid asthenosphere.

porosity. The proportion of void space (cracks, interstices) in a volume of a rock or sediment.

provenance. A place of origin. The area from which the constituent materials of a sedimentary rock were derived.

radioactivity. The spontaneous decay or breakdown of unstable atomic nuclei.

radiometric age. An age expressed in years and calculated from the quantitative determination of radioactive elements and their decay products.

recharge. Infiltration processes that replenish groundwater.

regression. A long-term seaward retreat of the shoreline or relative fall of sea level.

relative dating. Determining the chronological placement of rocks, events, or fossils with respect to the geologic time scale and without reference to their numerical age.

reverse fault. A contractional high-angle (greater than 45°) dip-slip fault in which the hanging wall moves up relative to the footwall (also see "thrust fault").

ripple marks. The undulating, approximately parallel and usually small-scale ridge pattern formed on sediment by the flow of wind or water.

sand. A clastic particle smaller than a granule and larger than a silt grain, having a diameter in the range of 1/16 mm (0.0025 in) to 2 mm (0.08 in).

sandstone. Clastic sedimentary rock of predominantly sand-sized grains.

sediment. An eroded and deposited, unconsolidated accumulation of rock and mineral fragments.

sedimentary rock. A consolidated and lithified rock consisting of clastic and/or chemical sediment(s). One of the three main classes of rocks—igneous, metamorphic, and sedimentary.

shale. A clastic sedimentary rock made of clay-sized particles that exhibit parallel splitting properties.

silt. Clastic sedimentary material intermediate in size between fine-grained sand and coarse clay (1/256 to 1/16 mm [0.00015 to 0.002 in]).

siltstone. A variably lithified sedimentary rock composed of silt-sized grains.

slump. A generally large, coherent mass movement with a concave-up failure surface and subsequent backward rotation relative to the slope.

stade. An interval of a glacial stage marked by a readvance of glaciers.

strata. Tabular or sheet-like masses or distinct layers of rock.

stratigraphy. The geologic study of the origin, occurrence, distribution, classification, correlation, and age of rock layers, especially sedimentary rocks.

stream. Any body of water moving under gravity flow in a clearly confined channel.

strike-slip fault. A fault with measurable offset where the relative movement is parallel to the strike of the fault.

Said to be "sinistral" (left-lateral) if relative motion of the block opposite the observer appears to be to the left. "Dextral" (right-lateral) describes relative motion to the right.

subduction zone. A convergent plate boundary where oceanic lithosphere descends beneath a continental or oceanic plate and is carried down into the mantle.

tectonic. Relating to large-scale movement and deformation of Earth's crust.

terrane. A large region or group of rocks with similar geology, age, or structural style.

terrestrial. Relating to land, Earth, or its inhabitants.

thrust fault. A contractional dip-slip fault with a shallowly dipping fault surface (less than 45°) where the hanging wall moves up and over relative to the footwall.

till. Unstratified drift, deposited directly by a glacier without reworking by meltwater, and consisting of a mixture of clay, silt, sand, gravel, and boulders ranging widely in size and shape.

topography. The general morphology of Earth's surface, including relief and locations of natural and anthropogenic features.

trace (fault). The exposed intersection of a fault with Earth's surface.

transgression. Landward migration of the sea as a result of a relative rise in sea level.

transpression. In crustal deformation, an intermediate stage between compression and strike-slip motion.

trend. The direction or azimuth of elongation of a linear geologic feature.

type locality. The geographic location where a stratigraphic unit (or fossil) is well displayed, formally defined, and derives its name. The place of original description.

unconformity. A substantial break or gap in the geologic record where a rock unit is overlain by another that is not next in stratigraphic succession.

volcanic. Describes anything related to volcanoes. Can refer to igneous rock crystallized at or near Earth's surface (e.g., lava).

volcaniclastic. Pertaining to all clastic volcanic materials formed by any process of fragmentation, dispersed by any kind of transporting agent, deposited in any environment, or mixed in any significant portion with nonvolcanic fragments.

water table. The upper surface of the saturated zone; the zone of rock in an aquifer saturated with water.

weathering. The physical, chemical, and biological processes by which rock is broken down.

Literature Cited

This section lists references cited in this report. A more complete geologic bibliography is available from the National Park Service Geologic Resources Division.

Atwater, B. F., and E. Hemphill-Haley. 1997. Recurrence intervals for great earthquakes of the past 3,500 years at northeastern Willapa Bay, Washington. Professional Paper 1576. U.S. Geological Survey, Reston, Virginia, USA. (http://pubs.usgs.gov/pp/1576/report.pdf). Accessed April 10, 2008.

Booth, D.B., J.G. Troost, J.J. Clague, and R.B. Waitt. 2004. The Cordilleran Ice Sheet. Pages 17–45 *in* A.R. Gillespie, S.C. Porter, and B.F. Atwater, editors. The Quaternary Period in the United States. Elsevier Ltd., San Francisco, California, USA.

Burns, R. 1985. The shape and form of Puget Sound. Washington Sea Grant Publication, University of Washington, Seattle, Washington, USA.

Bush, D. M., and R. Young. 2009. Coastal features and processes. Pages 47–67 *in* R. Young and L. Norby, editors. Geological monitoring. Geological Society of America, Boulder, Colorado, USA. (http://nature.nps.gov/geology/monitoring/coastal.cfm). Accessed September 19, 2011.

Canning, D. 2002. Climate change, climate variability, and sea level rise in Puget Sound: Possibilities for the future. *In* T. Droscher, editor. Proceedings of the 2001 Puget Sound Research Conference, Puget Sound Action Team, Olympia, Washington, USA.

Carlstad, C.A. 1992. Late Pleistocene deglaciation history at Point Partridge, central Whidbey Island, Washington. Thesis. Western Washington University, Bellingham, Washington, USA.

Dietrich, W. 2004. Whidbey's secret: Preserving the historic, the rural and the settled, together. The Seattle Times: Pacific Northwest Magazine. (http://seattletimes.nwsource.com/pacificnw/2004/061 3/cojver.html). Accessed April 10, 2008.

Domack, E.W. 1983. Facies of late Pleistocene glacial-marine sediments on Whidbey Island, Washington-- An isostatic glacial-marine sequence. Pages 535-570 *in* B.F. Molnia, editor, Glacial-marine sedimentation. Plenum Press, New York, New York, USA.

Dragovich, J.D., G.T. Petro, G.W. Thorsen, S.L. Larson, G.R. Foster, and D.K. Norman. 2005. Geologic map of the Oak Harbor, Crescent Harbor, and part of the Smith Island 7.5-minute quadrangles, Island County, Washington. Washington Division of Geology and Earth Resources, Geologic Map GM-59 (scale 1:24,000). (http://www.dnr.wa.gov/Publications/ger_gm59_geol_map_oakharbor_crescentharbor_24k.zip). Accessed September 19, 2011.

Easterbrook, D.J. 1994. Chronology of pre-late Wisconsin Pleistocene sediments in the Puget Lowland, Washington. Pages 191–206 *in* R. Lasmanis and E. S. Cheney, conveners. First symposium on the regional geology of Washington State. Washington Division of Geology and Earth Resources Bulletin 80, Olympia, Washington, USA.

Easterbrook, D.J., D.R. Crandell, and E.B. Leopold. 1967. Pre-Olympia Pleistocene stratigraphy and chronology in the central Puget Lowland, Washington. Geological Society of America Bulletin 78:13–20.

Easterbrook, D.J., K.L. Pierce, J. Gosse, A.R. Gillespie, E. Evenson, and K. Hamblin. 2003. Quaternary geology of the Western United States. Pages 19–79 *in* D. J. Easterbrook, editor. Quaternary geology of the United States. INQUA 2003 Field Guide Volume, XVIINQUA Congress. Desert Research Institute, Reno, Nevada, USA.

Fay, L.C., J.P. Kenworthy, and V.L. Santucci. 2009. Paleontological resource inventory and monitoring: North Coast and Cascades Network. Natural Resource Technical Report NPS/NRPC/NRTR-2009/250. Natural Resource Program Center, National Park Service, Fort Collins, Colorado, USA.

Gilbert, C.A. 1985. Ebey's Landing National Historical Reserve: Reading the cultural landscape. National Park Service, Pacific Northwest Region, Seattle, Washington, (http://www.nps.gov/archive/ebla/rcl/rcl.htm). Accessed March 28, 2011.

Gower, H.D. 1980. Bedrock geologic and quaternary tectonic map of the Port Townsend area, Washington. U.S. Geological Survey, Open-File Report 80–1174 (scale 1:100,000). (http://ngmdb.usgs.gov/Prodesc/proddesc_11492.htm). Accessed September 19, 2011.

Hebda, R.J., O. Lian, and S.R. Hicock. 2007. Environmental history of the mid Wisconsin Olympia Interstadial, Fraser Lowland, British Columbia, Canada. Geological Society of America, Abstracts with Programs 39(4):17.

Heusser, C.J., and L.E. Heusser. 1981. Palynology and paleotemperature analysis of the Whidbey Formation, Puget Lowland, Washington. Canadian Journal of Earth Sciences 18 (1): 136-149.

Johnson, S.Y., S.V. Dadisman, D.C. Mosher, R.J. Blakely, and J.R. Childs. 2001. Active tectonics of the Devils Mountain fault and related structures, northern Puget Lowland and eastern Strait of Juan de Fuca region, Pacific Northwest. Professional Paper 1643. U.S. Geological Survey, Reston, Virginia, USA. (http://pubs.usgs.gov/pp/p1643/). Accessed March 28, 2011.

Johnson, S.Y., A.R. Nelson, S.F. Personius, R.E. Wells, H.M. Kelsey, B.L. Sherrod, K. Okumura, R. Koehler, R. Witter, L.A. Bradley, and D.J. Harding. 2003. Maps and data from a trench investigation of the Utsalady Point Fault, Whidbey Island, Washington. U.S. Geological Survey, Miscellaneous Field Studies Map MF-2420. (http://pubs.usgs.gov/mf/2003/mf-2420/mf-2420-508.pdf). Accessed March 28, 2011.

Johnson, S.Y., C.J. Potter, J.M. Armentrout, J.J. Miller, C.A. Finn, and C.S. Weaver. 1996. The southern Whidbey Island fault: An active structure in the Puget Lowland, Washington. Geological Society of America, Bulletin 108.

Karl, T. R., J. M. Melillo, and T. C. Peterson, editors. 2009. Global climate change impacts in the United States. Cambridge University Press, Cambridge, United Kingdom. (http://www.globalchange.gov /usimpacts). Accessed June 2, 2010.

Kelsey, H.M., B. Sherrod, S.Y. Johnson, and S.V. Dadisman. 2004. Land-level changes from a late Holocene earthquake in the northern Puget Lowland, Washington. Geology 32 (6): 469–472.

Klinger, T., D. Fluharty, C. Byron, K. Evans, and J. Coyle. 2007. Assessment of coastal water resources and watershed conditions at Ebey's Landing National Historical Reserve (Washington). Natural Resource Technical Report NPS/NRWRD/NRTR-2007/369. Water Resources Division, Natural Resource Program Center, National Park Service, Fort Collins, Colorado, USA.

Keuler, R.F. 1988. Map showing coastal erosion, sediment supply, and longshore transport in the Port Townsend 30- by 60-minute quadrangle, Puget Sound region, Washington. Miscellaneous Investigation I-1198-E. U.S. Geological Survey, Reston, Virginia, USA.

Mustoe, G.E., and C.A. Carlstadt. 1995. A late Pleistocene brown bear (Ursus arctos) from northwest Washington. Northwest Science 9:106–113.

Mustoe, G.E., C.R. Harington, and R.E. Morlan. 2005. Cedar Hollow, an early Holocene faunal site from Whidbey Island, Washington. Western North American Naturalist 65 (4):429–440.

National Park Service. 2000. Ebey's Landing National Historical Reserve: Administrative history. U.S. Department of Interior, Washington, D.C., USA. (http://www.nps.gov/archive/ebla/adhi/adhi7.htm). Accessed March 28, 2011.

National Park Service. 2004. The National Parks: Index 2005–2007. U.S. Department of Interior, Washington, D.C., USA.

National Park Service. 2006. Ebey's Landing National Historical Reserve: Final general management plan and environmental impact statement. National Park Service, Pacific West Region, Seattle, Washington, USA. (http://www.nps.gov/ebla/parkmgmt/planning. htm). Accessed March 28, 2011.

National Park Service. 2008. Central Whidbey Island Archaeological Resources. Ebey's Landing National Historical Reserve, Coupeville, Washington, USA. (http://www.nps.gov/ebla/arhe/archaeology.htm) Accessed January 15, 2008.

National Park Service. 2011. Elwha River restoration. (http://www.nps.gov/olym/naturescience/elwha-ecosystem-restoration.htm). Accessed June 3, 2011.

National Oceanic and Atmospheric Administration. 2005. General NOAA Oil Monitoring Environment (GNOME). (http://response.restoration.noaa.gov/ software/gnome/gnome.html). Accessed June 7, 2011.

Polenz, M. 2005. A geologic field trip of the Ebey's Landing National Historical Reserve. Unpublished report, on file at Ebey's Landing National Historical Reserve.

Polenz, M., S.L. Slaughter, J.D. Dragovich, and G.W. Thorsen. 2005. Geologic map of the Ebey's Landing National Historical Reserve, Island County, Washington. Washington Division of Geology and Earth Resources, Open-File Report 2005-2 (scale 1;24,000). (http://wsldocs.sos.wa.gov/library/ docs/dnr/ofr05-2_2006_002116.pdf). Accessed September 19, 2011.

Satake, K., K. Shimazaki, Y. Tsuji, and K. Ueda. 1996. Time and size of a giant earthquake in Cascadia inferred from inferred from Japanese tsunami records of January 1700. Nature 379 (6562):246–249.

Satake, K., K. Wang, and B.F. Atwater. 2003. Fault slip and seismic moment of the 1700 Cascadia earthquake inferred from Japanese tsunami description. Journal of Geophysical Research 108 (B11):1–17.

Shipman, H. 2004. Coastal bluffs and sea cliffs on Puget Sound, Washington. Professional Paper 1693. U.S. Geological Survey, Reston, Virginia, USA. (http://www.ecy.wa.gov/pubs/o406029.pdf). Accessed June 2, 2011.

Troost, K.G. 2002. Summary of the Olympia nonglacial interval (MIS 3) in the Puget Lowland, Washington. Geological Society of America, Abstracts with Programs 34(5):109.

U.S. Geological Survey. 2008. Report: Is Glacier Peak a dangerous volcano? USGS Cascades Volcano Observatory webpage, Vancouver, Washington, USA. (http://vulcan.wr.usge.gov/Volcanoes/GlacierPeak/Hazards/OFR95-413/OFR95-413.html). Accessed May 26, 2011.

Wagner, H.C., and M.C. Wiley. 1980. Preliminary map of offshore geology in the Protection Island-Point Partridge area, northern Puget Sound, Washington. Open-File Report 80-548. U.S. Geological Survey, Reston, Virginia, USA. (http://ngmdb.usgs.gov/Prodesc/proddesc_11690.htm). Accessed September 19, 2011.

Waitt, R.B., L.G. Mastin, and J.E. Beget. 1995. Volcanic-hazard zonation for Glacier Peak volcano, Washington. Open-file Report 95-499. U.S. Geological Survey, Reston, Virginia, USA. (http://vulcan.wr.usgs.gov/Volcanoes/GlacierPeak/Hazards). Accessed May 27, 2011.

Walsh, T.J., V.V. Titov, A.J. Venturato, H.O. Mofjeld, and F.I. Gonzalez. 2005. Tsunami hazard map of the Anacortes-Whidbey Island area, Washington: Modeled tsunami inundation from a Cascadia Subduction Zone earthquake. Washington Department of Natural Resources Open-File Report 2005-1 (scale 1:62,500). (http://www.dnr.wa.gov/Publications/ger_ofr2005-1_tsunami_hazard_anacortes_whidbey.pdf). Accessed September 19, 2011.

Washington State Department of Ecology. 2003. Admiralty Inlet/Hood Canal: Geographic response plan. (http://www.ecy.wa.gov/programs/spills/preparedness/grp/admiralty%20inlet-hood%20canal%20pdf/ai-hc%20grp%20intro%203-03%20f.pdf). Accessed June 7, 2011.

Washington State Department of Natural Resources. 2010. Geology of Washington: Puget Lowland. (http://www.dnr.wa.gov/ResearchScience/Topics/GeologyofWashington/Pages/lowland.aspx). Accessed July 14, 2010.

Wieczorek, G.F., and J.B. Snyder. 2009. Monitoring slope movements. Pages 245–271 in R. Young and L. Norby, editors. Geological monitoring. Geological Society of America, Boulder, Colorado, USA. (http://nature.nps.gov/geology/monitoring/slopes.cfm). Accessed September 19, 2011.

Additional References

This section lists additional references, resources, and web sites that may be of use to resource managers. Web addresses are current as of September 2011.

Geology of National Park Service Areas

National Park Service Geologic Resources Division (Lakewood, Colorado). http://nature.nps.gov/geology/

NPS Geologic Resources Inventory. http://www.nature.nps.gov/geology/inventory/gre_publications.cfm

Harris, A. G., E. Tuttle, and S. D. Tuttle. 2003. Geology of National Parks. Sixth Edition. Kendall/Hunt Publishing Co., Dubuque, Iowa, USA.

Kiver, E. P. and D. V. Harris. 1999. Geology of U.S. parklands. John Wiley and Sons, Inc., New York, New York, USA.

Lillie, R. J. 2005. Parks and Plates: The geology of our national parks, monuments, and seashores. W.W. Norton and Co., New York, New York, USA. [Geared for interpreters].

NPS Geoscientist-in-the-parks (GIP) internship and guest scientist program. http://www.nature.nps.gov/geology/gip/index.cfm

Resource Management/Legislation Documents

NPS 2006 Management Policies (Chapter 4; Natural Resource Management): http://www.nps.gov/policy/mp/policies.html#_Toc157232681

NPS-75: Natural Resource Inventory and Monitoring Guideline: http://www.nature.nps.gov/nps75/nps75.pdf

NPS Natural Resource Management Reference Manual #77: http://www.nature.nps.gov/Rm77/

Geologic Monitoring Manual
R. Young and L. Norby, editors. Geological Monitoring. Geological Society of America, Boulder, Colorado. http://nature.nps.gov/geology/monitoring/index.cfm

NPS Technical Information Center (Denver, repository for technical (TIC) documents): http://etic.nps.gov/

Geological Survey and Society Websites

Washington State Department of Natural Resources. http://www.dnr.wa.gov/Pages/default.aspx

U.S. Geological Survey: http://www.usgs.gov/

Geological Society of America: http://www.geosociety.org/

American Geological Institute: http://www.agiweb.org/

Association of American State Geologists: http://www.stategeologists.org/

Other Geology/Resource Management Tools

Bates, R. L. and J. A. Jackson, editors. American Geological Institute dictionary of geological terms (3rd Edition). Bantam Doubleday Dell Publishing Group, New York.

U.S. Geological Survey National Geologic Map Database (NGMDB): http://ngmdb.usgs.gov/

U.S. Geological Survey Geologic Names Lexicon (GEOLEX; geologic unit nomenclature and summary): http://ngmdb.usgs.gov/Geolex/geolex_home.html

U.S. Geological Survey Geographic Names Information System (GNIS; search for place names and geographic features, and plot them on topographic maps or aerial photos): http://gnis.usgs.gov/

U.S. Geological Survey GeoPDFs (download searchable PDFs of any topographic map in the United States): http://store.usgs.gov (click on "Map Locator").

U.S. Geological Survey Publications Warehouse (many USGS publications are available online): http://pubs.er.usgs.gov

U.S. Geological Survey, description of physiographic provinces: http://tapestry.usgs.gov/Default.html

Appendix: Scoping Session Participants

The following is a list of participants from the GRI scoping session for Ebey's Landing National Historical Reserve, held on September 10-12, 2002. The contact information and email addresses in this appendix may be outdated; please contact the Geologic Resources Division for current information. The scoping meeting summary was used as the foundation for this GRI report. The original scoping summary document is available on the GRI publications web site:
http://www.nature.nps.gov/geology/inventory/gre_publications.cfm.

Name	Affiliation	Position	Phone	E-mail
Andrascik, Roger	NPS – Voyageurs National Park	Natural Resources	218-283-9821	Roger_Andrascik@nps.gov
Beavers, Rebecca	NPS – Geological Resources Division	Geologist	303-987-6945	rebecca_beavers@nps.gov
Connors, Tim	NPS - Geological Resources Division	Geologist	303-969-2093	tim_Connors@nps.gov
Dalby, Craig	NPS - CCSO	GIS	206-220-4261	craig_dalby@nps.gov
Davis, Marsha	NPS – Northwest Network	Geologist		Marsha_Davis@nps.gov
Doyle, Rebecca	NPS – Mount Rainier National Park	Biologist	360-569-2211	rebecca_doyle@nps.gov
Graham, John	Colorado State University	Geologist		
Haugerud, Ralph	U.S. Geological Survey	Geologist	206-553-5542	rhaguerud@usgs.gov
Heise, Bruce	NPS - Geological Resources Division	Geologist	303-969-2017	Bruce_Heise@nps.gov
Latham, Penny	NPS - CCSO	PWR IM	206-220-4267	penny_latham@nps.gov
Norman, Dave	WA Department of Natural Resources	Geologist	360-902-1439	dave.Norman@wadnr.gov
Pringle, Pat	WA Department of Natural Resources	Geologist	360-902-1433	pat.pringle@wadnr.gov
Riedel, Jon	NPS – North Cascades National Park	Geologist	360-873-4590	jon_riedel@nps.gov
Samora, Barbara	NPS – Mount Rainier National Park	Natural Resources	360-569-2211	barbara_samora@nps.gov
Swinney, Darin	NPS – Mount Rainier National Park	GIS	360-569-2211	darin_swinney@nps.gov
Teissere, Ron	WA Division of Natural Resources	Geologist	360-902-1440	ron.teissere@wadnr.gov

NPS 484/110343, September 2011